PROBLEM-BASED LEARNING
THE HANDBOOK FOR
INSTRUCTORS AND SCHOLARS

Copyright

The contents of this book, including but not limited to text, images, and illustrations, are protected under the copyright laws of United States of America and international conventions. The author and publisher have made every effort to ensure that the information provided in this book is accurate and up to date at the time of publication.

Unauthorized reproduction or distribution of any part of this book is prohibited. This includes but is not limited to copying, scanning, or distributing in any form or by any means, including electronic, mechanical, photocopying, recording, or otherwise, without the prior written permission of the author and publisher.

Copyright © 2023

Dr. Lester Reid

ISBN: 978-1-7340601-2-6

Global Higher Education Institute Publishing

ACKNOWLEDGEMENT

I would like to take this opportunity to express my deepest gratitude and appreciation to the many individuals who have supported me throughout the journey of writing this book. Their unwavering encouragement, guidance, and love have been instrumental in bringing this project to fruition.

First and foremost, I want to extend my heartfelt thanks to my beloved son. Your constant support, understanding, and patience have been a constant source of inspiration for me. Your belief in my abilities and the countless discussions we have had about the ideas in this book have enriched my perspective and motivated me to give my best. I am incredibly proud to have you as my son, and I am grateful for the love we share.

To my esteemed clients, thank you for entrusting me with the opportunity to work with you. Your collaboration and feedback have been invaluable in shaping my understanding of the topics covered in this book. It is your real-life experiences and challenges that have enriched the content and made it relevant and practical.

I would also like to express my gratitude to the higher education institutions I have been fortunate to work for. The supportive environments, resources, and opportunities they provided have been instrumental in fostering my growth as an educator and researcher. I am indebted to the faculty, staff, and administration for their mentorship and belief in my abilities.

To my graduate and undergraduate students, you have been the driving force behind my passion for teaching and learning. Your curiosity, dedication, and willingness to challenge yourselves have inspired me to continually improve and innovate in my pedagogy. It has been an honor to be part of your academic journeys, and I am grateful for the opportunity to have contributed to your educational development.

Last but not least, I want to express my deepest gratitude to my parents. Your unwavering love, encouragement, and belief in me have been the foundation of my personal and professional achievements. I am forever grateful for your sacrifices, guidance, and the values you instilled in me.

To all those mentioned here and the countless others who have touched my life, I offer my heartfelt thanks. This book would not have been possible without your presence and support. Your contributions have played an integral role in shaping both my personal and professional journey. Thank you for being a part of my life and for the love and support you have shown me.

ABOUT THIS BOOK

In recent years, there has been a growing interest in student-centered approaches to education that foster critical thinking, problem-solving skills, and deep learning. Problem-based learning (PBL) has emerged as an effective pedagogical strategy that engages learners in active inquiry and problem-solving processes. This book explores the principles, methods, and benefits of PBL, highlighting relevant research from the past three years.

Problem-based learning offers a student-centered approach to education that promotes active learning, critical thinking, and collaborative skills. By engaging students in authentic problem-solving experiences, PBL prepares them for the challenges of the real world and encourages lifelong learning. This book has provided an overview of PBL, its design and implementation, cognitive and metacognitive processes, social and emotional aspects, its applications in STEM fields, integration of technology, and assessment strategies. As education continues to evolve, problem-based learning holds great potential to foster deep learning and empower students to become lifelong learners and problem solvers.

At the heart of problem-based learning lies the notion of relevance. By framing learning within real-world contexts, PBL bridges the gap between theory and practice, enabling students to see the direct applications of their knowledge. Whether it's exploring environmental sustainability, designing innovative technologies, or addressing social inequities, PBL provides a platform for students to engage with meaningful and pressing issues. This approach not only enhances their motivation and engagement but also prepares them to become active contributors to society, equipped with the skills needed to effect positive change.

One of the key strengths of problem-based learning is its emphasis on collaboration and teamwork. In PBL settings, students work in small groups, pooling their diverse perspectives, expertise, and experiences to tackle complex problems. Through collaboration, students learn to appreciate the value of multiple viewpoints, develop effective communication skills, and cultivate empathy—a crucial attribute in today's globalized world. By working together, students discover the power of collective intelligence and gain invaluable skills that will serve them well beyond the classroom.

Table of Contents

PREFACE **12**

CHAPTER ONE **15**

   Understanding Problem-Based Learning **15**
      Defining Problem-Based Learning 18
      Historical Development of PBL 18
      Key Features and Components of PBL 19
      PBL in Various Educational Contexts 21

CHAPTER TWO **30**

   Designing and Implementing PBL **30**
      Identifying Authentic and Challenging Problems 30
      Formulating Problem Statements 31
      A common structure for PBL units includes the following key components: 33
      Facilitating Group Dynamics and Collaboration 35
      Educators can foster positive group dynamics and collaboration through the following strategies: 36
      Role of the Instructor in PBL 37
      The instructor's role in PBL includes: 37
      Assessing PBL Outcomes 38
      Here are some assessment methods suitable for PBL: 39
      The True Benefactors of Problem Based Learning 43

CHAPTER THREE **48**

   Cognitive and Metacognitive Processes in PBL **48**
      Inquiry and Critical Thinking Skills 50
      Self-Directed Learning 51
      Reflection and Metacognition 52
      Problem-Solving Strategies in PBL 53

CHAPTER FOUR **64**

   Collaboration and Communication Skills **64**
      Teamwork and Interpersonal Relationships 65

Motivation and Engagement 67
Student Ownership and Autonomy 68
Emotional Intelligence in PBL 70

CHAPTER FIVE 79

PBL in Science, Technology, Engineering, and Mathematics (STEM) 79
PBL in Science Education 79
PBL in Technology Education 81
PBL in Engineering Education 83
PBL in Mathematics Education 85
Integration of STEM Disciplines in PBL 88

CHAPTER SIX 101

Technology and Problem-Based Learning 101
Digital Tools and Resources for PBL 101
Online and Virtual PBL Environments 102
Blended Approaches to PBL 103
Challenges and Opportunities in Technology-Enhanced PBL 103
Online Collaboration Tools 105
Multimedia Resources 106
Online Research and Information Literacy 107
Digital Portfolios and Reflection 108
Online Discussion Forums and Blogs 109
Mobile Devices and Apps 109
Data Visualization Tools 110

Problem-Based Learning Application in Industries 111
Healthcare Industry 111
Environmental Conservation 112
Engineering and Construction 112
Business and Entrepreneurship 112
Education and E-Learning 113
Manufacturing and Robotics 113
Agriculture and Food Production 114
Renewable Energy 114
Transportation and Logistics 115

Entertainment and Media 115

CHAPTER SEVEN 117

Assessment and Evaluation in PBL 117
   Authentic Assessment Methods 117
   Rubrics and Criteria for PBL 119
   Assessing Collaborative Skills and Individual Contributions
   121
   Feedback and Reflection on Learning 123
   Evaluating the Impact of PBL 125

When and Where Assessment Evaluation Takes Place .. 128

CHAPTER EIGHT 138

How to Implement PBL into the classroom 138
   Benefits of Introducing PBL in K-12 Education 148
   Considerations for Implementing PBL in K-12 Education 149
   Benefits of Introducing PBL in Higher Education 150

CHAPTER NINE 154

Problem-Based Learning in Disciplines 154
   Problem-Based Learning in Teaching 154
   Problem-Based Learning in Accounting and Finance 155
   Problem-Based Learning in Data Analytics 155
   Problem-Based Learning in Business Management 156
   Problem-Based Learning in Economics 157
   Problem-Based Learning in Engineering 157
   Problem-Based Learning in Higher Education
   Administration 158
   Problem-Based Learning in Computer Science 158
   Problem-Based Learning in Psychology 159
   Problem-Based Learning in Communications 159
   Problem Based Learning – By College Major 161

Underutilization of Problem-Based Learning in the
Classroom 166

Improving the Utilization of Problem-Based Learning by Professors 176

CHAPTER TEN *184*

Foundation Theorists of Problem Based Learning 184

The Value and Appreciation of Problem-Based Learning Theorists' Work 196

CHAPTER ELEVEN *202*

Problem Based Learning in the Work Environment 202

The Principles and Methodologies of PBL 206

Sixty Reasons to Apply PBL in the Workplace 211

Problem-Based Learning (PBL) Application in Departments Within an Organization 217

1. Accounting: 218
2. Finance: 218
3. Human Resources: 219
4. Strategic Management: 220
5. Marketing: 221
6. Project Management: 221
7. Supply Chain Management: 222

US and Inter'l Universities Implemented PBL *224*

PREFACE

Welcome to this exploration of problem-based learning (PBL), a pedagogical approach that has gained recognition and popularity in educational settings worldwide. As educators and learners, we constantly seek innovative methods to enhance our understanding, critical thinking skills, and real-world application of knowledge. In this pursuit, problem-based learning emerges as a compelling solution, engaging students in meaningful problem-solving experiences that bridge the gap between theory and practice.

Traditional educational models often focus on the transmission of knowledge from teacher to student, emphasizing rote memorization and passive learning. While these methods have their merits, they can sometimes fail to instill deeper comprehension, creativity, and the ability to tackle complex, authentic challenges. This is where problem-based learning steps in, revolutionizing the way we teach and learn by centering the educational process around real-world problems.

At its core, problem-based learning is a student-centered approach that places learners in the driver's seat of their own education. Rather than relying solely on lectures and textbooks, PBL encourages students to actively engage with problems that reflect the complexity of the world they will encounter beyond the classroom walls. These problems, carefully designed and aligned with the curriculum, serve as catalysts for deep learning, critical thinking, collaboration, and the application of knowledge in authentic contexts.

In a problem-based learning environment, learners become active participants in their own learning journey. They are challenged to investigate and explore relevant, multifaceted problems that require interdisciplinary thinking, creativity, and problem-solving skills. PBL cultivates a deep sense of ownership over one's education, empowering students to develop a growth mindset and take responsibility for their learning outcomes.

Throughout this book, we will examine the various dimensions and benefits of problem-based learning. We will examine how PBL nurtures essential 21st-century skills, including critical thinking, communication, collaboration, and creativity. By immersing ourselves in the world of PBL, we will discover how it promotes a deep understanding of subject matter, encourages inquiry and research skills, and fosters a lifelong love of learning.

One of the key strengths of problem-based learning lies in its ability to simulate authentic, real-world situations. By grappling with complex problems, students develop a deep understanding of the interconnectedness of knowledge across disciplines. They learn to navigate ambiguity and uncertainty, honing their ability to identify relevant information, analyze data, and make informed decisions. Through collaboration and teamwork, learners experience the richness of diverse perspectives and develop strong interpersonal skills that are crucial for success in the modern world.

CHAPTER ONE
Understanding Problem-Based Learning

In recent years, there has been a growing interest in student-centered approaches to education that foster critical thinking, problem-solving skills, and deep learning. Problem-based learning (PBL) has emerged as an effective pedagogical strategy that engages learners in active inquiry and problem-solving processes. This book explores the principles, methods, and benefits of PBL, highlighting relevant research from the past three years.

Problem-based learning offers a student-centered approach to education that promotes active learning, critical thinking, and collaborative skills. By engaging students in authentic problem-solving experiences, PBL prepares them for the challenges of the real world and encourages lifelong learning. This book has provided an overview of PBL, its design and implementation, cognitive and metacognitive processes, social and emotional aspects, its applications in STEM fields, integration of technology, and assessment strategies. As education continues to evolve, problem-based learning holds great potential to foster deep learning and empower students to become lifelong learners and problem solvers.

As we navigate the complexities and uncertainties of the 21st century, problem-based learning offers a transformative approach to education. By equipping students with the skills, knowledge, and attitudes necessary for success in an ever-changing world, PBL prepares them to become active contributors, critical thinkers, and compassionate problem solvers. It fosters a love for learning, encourages curiosity, and nurtures a growth mindset. By embracing problem-based learning, we are paving the way for a future where education is not just about acquiring information but about developing the skills and dispositions to shape a better world.

As educators, it is our responsibility to cultivate a learning environment that prepares students for the challenges they will face beyond the classroom. Problem-based learning offers an ideal platform to equip learners with the skills and dispositions necessary to thrive in an ever-changing society. By engaging in PBL, students become active agents of change, capable of applying their knowledge and skills to solve real-world problems, contribute to their communities, and shape a better future.

In the pages that follow, we will explore the principles, strategies, and best practices of problem-based learning. We will encounter inspiring stories of educators and learners who have experienced the transformative power of PBL firsthand. We will examine the process of designing and implementing effective PBL units and discover the tools and resources available to support this pedagogical approach. Together, we will embark on a journey of exploration, innovation, and growth, as we unlock the immense potential of problem-based learning.

Let us embrace the power of problem-based learning and embark on a transformative educational journey that transcends traditional boundaries. Together, we can create learning experiences that ignite curiosity, empower learners, and equip them with the skills they need to navigate the complexities of the world.

Are you ready to embrace the challenges and opportunities that await? Let us embark on this PBL adventure together!

Defining Problem-Based Learning

Problem-Based Learning (PBL) is an educational approach that emphasizes the active engagement of learners in solving real-world problems. It is a student-centered pedagogy that focuses on the development of critical thinking, problem-solving skills, and collaboration. In PBL, learners are presented with authentic, ill-structured problems that require them to identify relevant information, analyze the problem, generate hypotheses, and develop solutions. This approach encourages students to become independent, lifelong learners who can apply their knowledge in practical settings.

Historical Development of PBL

The origins of PBL can be traced back to the medical education field. In the 1960s, McMaster University in Canada introduced a new medical curriculum that departed from the traditional lecture-based approach. The faculty recognized the need to train doctors who could think critically and apply their knowledge in clinical practice. This led to the development of the problem-based learning model, which aimed to integrate basic science knowledge with clinical practice through the use of authentic patient cases.

Since its inception in medical education, PBL has gained popularity and has been adapted in various disciplines and educational contexts. The success of PBL in medical education paved the way for its application in fields such as engineering, business, law, and education. The underlying principles of PBL, which include active learning, self-directedness, and problem-solving, align with the demands of the 21st-century workforce and the need for individuals who can adapt to complex and dynamic environments.

Key Features and Components of PBL

Authentic Problems: PBL revolves around the use of authentic, ill-structured problems that reflect real-world challenges. These problems are designed to engage learners and require them to apply their existing knowledge and skills to develop meaningful solutions. Authentic problems enhance the relevance of learning and promote the transfer of knowledge to practical contexts.

Student-Centeredness: PBL places students at the center of the learning process. Instead of relying on teachers to transmit knowledge, students take an active role in defining their learning goals, identifying information gaps, and seeking out resources to address those gaps. This student-centered approach promotes self-directed learning, autonomy, and responsibility for one's own education.

Collaborative Learning: Collaboration is a fundamental component of PBL. Students work together in small groups to explore the problem, share ideas, discuss different perspectives, and construct knowledge collectively. Collaborative learning fosters teamwork, communication skills, and the ability to work effectively in diverse groups.

Facilitator Role: In PBL, the role of the teacher shifts from being a knowledge provider to that of a facilitator. The facilitator guides students in the process of problem-solving, provides support and resources, and promotes reflection and metacognitive skills. The facilitator's role is to create a supportive learning environment and to scaffold students' learning experiences.

Reflection and Metacognition: PBL encourages learners to reflect on their thinking processes, problem-solving strategies, and learning experiences. Reflection and metacognition help students develop a deeper understanding of the subject matter and enhance their ability to transfer knowledge to new situations. Regular reflection fosters self-awareness, critical thinking, and continuous improvement.

PBL in Various Educational Contexts

PBL has been successfully implemented in various educational contexts, ranging from K-12 schools to higher education and professional development settings. Here are a few examples of how PBL has been adapted in different domains:

K-12 Education: PBL has gained popularity in K-12 schools as a means to engage students in meaningful learning experiences. By presenting authentic problems, students develop critical thinking, creativity, and collaboration skills. PBL aligns with the principles of constructivism and inquiry-based learning, enabling students to take ownership of their learning and develop a deep understanding of the subject matter.

Higher Education: PBL has been widely adopted in higher education institutions across various disciplines. In addition to medical education, PBL is commonly used in fields such as engineering, business, and law. It provides students with opportunities to apply theoretical concepts to real-world problems, enhancing their problem-solving abilities and preparing them for professional practice.

Professional Development: PBL has also found applications in professional development programs for educators and professionals. By engaging participants in authentic problems relevant to their field, PBL promotes the acquisition of practical skills, critical thinking, and reflective practice. PBL in professional development settings encourages continuous learning and the transfer of knowledge and skills to real-world contexts.

Online and Blended Learning: With the increasing prevalence of online and blended learning environments, PBL has been adapted to suit these contexts. Virtual platforms and online resources provide opportunities for students to collaborate, access information, and engage in authentic problem-solving activities. Online PBL promotes flexibility, personalized learning, and the development of digital literacy skills.

Problem-Based Learning (PBL) is an educational approach that fosters active learning, critical thinking, and problem-solving skills. PBL originated in medical education and has since been adapted and implemented in various educational contexts. Key features of PBL include the use of authentic problems, student-centeredness, collaborative learning, facilitator roles, and reflection. PBL has proven to be effective in engaging learners, promoting deeper understanding, and preparing individuals for real-world challenges in diverse fields. As education continues to evolve, PBL offers a valuable framework for cultivating the skills and competencies needed in the 21st century.

Problem-Based Learning (PBL) is an educational approach that has the potential to make lives better by equipping individuals with the necessary skills, knowledge, and attitudes to address real-world problems and improve their personal and professional lives. PBL offers a learner-centered, active learning experience that goes beyond rote memorization and passive learning. This book explores how Problem-Based Learning can positively impact lives and contribute to personal growth and development.

One way in which Problem-Based Learning enhances lives is by fostering critical thinking and problem-solving skills. PBL encourages individuals to analyze complex problems, consider multiple perspectives, and develop innovative solutions. This ability to think critically and approach challenges with a problem-solving mindset is invaluable in various aspects of life. Whether it's solving personal dilemmas, making informed decisions, or tackling professional obstacles, individuals trained in PBL are better equipped to navigate the complexities of everyday life and achieve positive outcomes.

Moreover, Problem-Based Learning promotes lifelong learning. In today's rapidly evolving world, the ability to adapt, learn new skills, and stay updated with the latest developments is crucial. PBL cultivates a sense of curiosity, self-directed learning, and a passion for acquiring knowledge. Individuals engaged in PBL develop the skills to seek out information, evaluate its credibility, and apply it in practical settings. This empowers individuals to continuously learn and grow, not only during their formal education but throughout their lives. By fostering a culture of lifelong learning, PBL ensures that individuals remain relevant, adaptable, and capable of seizing new opportunities.

Problem-Based Learning also has a positive impact on personal and professional relationships. PBL often involves collaborative group work, where individuals from diverse backgrounds come together to solve problems. Through this process, individuals develop strong communication, teamwork, and interpersonal skills. They learn to listen actively, respect different viewpoints, and collaborate effectively. These skills are invaluable in personal relationships, enabling individuals to build strong connections, resolve conflicts, and work towards common goals. In professional settings, individuals trained in PBL excel in team environments, contribute to a positive work culture, and enhance productivity through effective collaboration.

Furthermore, Problem-Based Learning nurtures creativity and innovation. PBL encourages individuals to think outside the box, explore unconventional ideas, and develop innovative solutions to problems. This fosters a mindset of creativity, encouraging individuals to challenge the status quo and seek alternative approaches. In personal lives, this creativity can manifest in finding unique solutions to everyday challenges, pursuing hobbies and passions, and thinking creatively about personal growth and development.

Professionally, individuals trained in PBL bring fresh perspectives, generate innovative ideas, and drive positive change within their organizations.

Problem-Based Learning also promotes empathy and social responsibility. PBL often incorporates real-world problems that require individuals to consider ethical implications, social justice, and the impact of their actions on others. This cultivates a sense of empathy, compassion, and a desire to contribute positively to society. Individuals trained in PBL develop a strong sense of social responsibility, actively seeking solutions that address social, environmental, and economic challenges. Whether it's volunteering, engaging in community projects, or advocating for positive change, individuals with a PBL background are more likely to make meaningful contributions to their communities.

Moreover, Problem-Based Learning can have a positive impact on personal and professional confidence. Through the process of actively engaging in problem-solving and finding solutions, individuals develop a sense of accomplishment and self-assurance.

They gain confidence in their abilities to tackle challenges, overcome obstacles, and achieve success. This newfound confidence extends beyond the realm of problem-solving and permeates other areas of life, empowering individuals to take on new opportunities, face adversity with resilience, and pursue their goals with determination.

Problem-Based Learning has the potential to make lives better by equipping individuals with critical thinking, problem-solving skills, a thirst for lifelong learning, and a sense of social responsibility. By fostering creativity, collaboration, and empathy, PBL enhances personal and professional relationships and promotes positive change in society. The skills and attitudes developed through PBL enable individuals to navigate life's challenges, seize opportunities, and contribute meaningfully to their communities. As educators and learners continue to embrace Problem-Based Learning, the potential to make lives better becomes increasingly evident.

CHAPTER TWO
Designing and Implementing PBL

Problem-Based Learning (PBL) is an instructional approach that promotes student-centered learning through the exploration and resolution of real-world problems. In this chapter, we will examine the various aspects of designing and implementing PBL, including identifying authentic and challenging problems, formulating problem statements, structuring PBL units, facilitating group dynamics and collaboration, understanding the role of the instructor in PBL, and assessing PBL outcomes.

Identifying Authentic and Challenging Problems

One of the crucial steps in designing a successful PBL unit is identifying authentic and challenging problems. These problems should be relevant to the students' lives and have real-world applications. Authentic problems are those that reflect the complexities and uncertainties of the real world, requiring students to apply their knowledge and skills in meaningful ways. Challenging problems push students to think critically, engage in problem-solving, and seek multiple perspectives.

To identify authentic and challenging problems, educators can draw from various sources such as current events, local community issues, professional contexts, or interdisciplinary topics. They can also collaborate with experts from relevant fields to ensure the problems align with real-world challenges. By presenting students with meaningful problems, educators can stimulate their curiosity and motivation to explore and understand the subject matter deeply.

Formulating Problem Statements

Once the authentic and challenging problems are identified, the next step is formulating problem statements. A problem statement should clearly define the problem, provide sufficient context, and outline the desired outcomes. It should be open-ended, allowing for multiple solutions and encouraging students to explore different approaches.

Effective problem statements should also consider the students' prior knowledge and skills, ensuring that the problems are within their reach while still being challenging enough to promote learning and growth. The problem statements should be concise, focused, and relevant to the overall learning objectives of the PBL unit.

Educators can collaborate with their colleagues or engage students in the process of formulating problem statements. Involving students in this process empowers them to take ownership of their learning and fosters a sense of relevance and authenticity.

Structuring PBL Units

Structuring PBL units involves organizing the learning activities, resources, and assessments in a coherent and sequential manner. A well-structured PBL unit provides students with a clear roadmap for their learning journey.

A common structure for PBL units includes the following key components:

1. *Introduction:* Introduce the problem and its relevance to the students. Help them develop an understanding of the problem's context and importance.
2. *Inquiry and Research:* Encourage students to explore the problem, ask questions, and conduct research. Provide them with the necessary resources and guidance to gather information and develop a deeper understanding.
3. *Group Work and Collaboration:* Facilitate group work, where students can collaborate, brainstorm ideas, and develop solutions together. Group work promotes teamwork, communication, and the sharing of diverse perspectives.
4. *Problem Solving and Solution Development:* Guide students in analyzing the problem, identifying possible solutions, and designing a plan of action. Encourage critical thinking and creative problem-solving strategies.
5. *Presentation and Reflection:* Provide opportunities for students to present their

solutions to the class or a wider audience. Reflection activities allow students to evaluate their learning process, reflect on their growth, and identify areas for improvement.

By structuring PBL units in a coherent and logical manner, educators can support students in navigating through the complexities of the problem and scaffold their learning effectively. One of the significant advantages of Problem-Based Learning is its ability to bridge the gap between theory and practice. Traditional education often relies on lectures and passive learning, which may not adequately prepare individuals for real-world challenges. However, PBL offers a hands-on, experiential learning environment where individuals are confronted with complex problems similar to those encountered in their respective professions. By actively engaging in problem-solving activities, students develop critical thinking, analytical reasoning, and decision-making skills that are highly transferable to the workplace.

Facilitating Group Dynamics and Collaboration

Collaboration and group work are essential components of PBL. Students working in teams learn to communicate effectively, leverage each other's strengths, and develop valuable interpersonal skills. However, effective group dynamics require intentional facilitation. Problem-Based Learning also fosters collaboration and teamwork, which are vital skills in most job settings. PBL often involves group work, where individuals work together to analyze, discuss, and find solutions to the given problems. This collaborative approach promotes effective communication, conflict resolution, and the ability to work effectively in diverse teams. Such skills are highly valued by employers, as they contribute to a positive work culture and enhance productivity within organizations.

Educators can foster positive group dynamics and collaboration through the following strategies:

1. *Establishing Clear Expectations:* Set clear expectations for collaboration, emphasizing respect, active listening, and equal participation. Establish norms for decision-making and conflict resolution.
2. *Providing Guidance and Support:* Offer guidance on effective teamwork strategies, communication skills, and conflict resolution techniques. Encourage students to take responsibility for their roles within the group.
3. *Monitoring and Facilitating:* Observe group interactions, provide feedback, and intervene when necessary. Address any issues or conflicts that may arise, ensuring an inclusive and supportive learning environment.
4. *Promoting Reflection:* Encourage students to reflect on their group dynamics, collaboration process, and individual contributions. Reflection activities can help students identify areas

for improvement and enhance their teamwork skills.

Role of the Instructor in PBL

In a PBL environment, the role of the instructor shifts from being a traditional content deliverer to that of a facilitator and guide. The instructor's primary responsibility is to support and guide students in their learning process.

The instructor's role in PBL includes:

1. *Setting the Stage:* Introduce the problem, provide necessary background information, and engage students' interest. Help students understand the relevance of the problem and its connection to the learning objectives.
2. *Guiding Inquiry:* Facilitate students' inquiry process by posing thought-provoking questions, suggesting research resources, and encouraging critical thinking. The instructor guides students to find answers, rather than providing them directly.
3. *Monitoring Progress:* Monitor students' progress and provide timely feedback.

Assess individual and group understanding, offer guidance, and identify areas where students may need additional support.
4. ***Facilitating Discussions:*** Engage students in discussions that promote deeper thinking, reflection, and the exchange of ideas. Encourage students to ask questions, challenge assumptions, and explore different perspectives.
5. ***Supporting Reflection and Metacognition:*** Promote reflection on the learning process, helping students develop metacognitive skills. Encourage self-assessment and goal-setting, enabling students to take ownership of their learning.

The instructor's role is to create a supportive learning environment that encourages student autonomy, collaboration, and critical thinking.

Assessing PBL Outcomes

Assessing PBL outcomes involves evaluating students' understanding, problem-solving abilities, and collaboration skills. Traditional assessment methods like exams and quizzes may not fully capture the multifaceted nature of PBL. Therefore, alternative assessment strategies are necessary. Another significant outcome of Problem-Based Learning on the job is the development of problem-solving and adaptability skills. In a rapidly changing professional landscape, individuals need to be adept at identifying and addressing complex problems effectively. PBL equips learners with the ability to navigate uncertain situations, think creatively, and adapt their strategies as needed. These skills are crucial in various professions, where individuals must constantly find innovative solutions to challenges and stay ahead of evolving trends.

Here are some assessment methods suitable for PBL:

1. *Performance Assessments:* Assess students' ability to apply their knowledge and skills to real-world problems. Performance assessments can include presentations, portfolios, case studies, simulations, or product creations.

2. ***Rubrics and Checklists:*** Develop rubrics and checklists that outline the criteria for successful problem-solving and collaboration. Rubrics provide clear expectations and allow for consistent and objective assessment.
3. ***Peer and Self-Assessment:*** Encourage students to assess their own work and the work of their peers. Peer and self-assessment promote critical thinking, metacognition, and provide students with valuable feedback.
4. ***Reflection and Journals:*** Incorporate reflection activities and journal writing as part of the assessment process. Reflection allows students to articulate their learning process, identify challenges, and reflect on their growth.
5. ***Feedback and Formative Assessment:*** Provide ongoing feedback throughout the PBL unit to guide students' progress. Use formative assessment strategies to identify areas where students may need additional support.

Assessment in PBL should focus on the process of learning, students' growth, and their ability to transfer knowledge and skills to authentic contexts. It should encourage students to demonstrate their understanding and application of concepts in real-world problem-solving scenarios. Designing and implementing PBL requires careful consideration of authentic and challenging problems, formulating problem statements, structuring PBL units, facilitating group dynamics and collaboration, understanding the role of the instructor, and assessing PBL outcomes. By incorporating these elements effectively, educators can create engaging and meaningful learning experiences that promote critical thinking, problem-solving, and collaboration skills in students.

Problem-Based Learning enhances individuals' self-directed learning capabilities. PBL encourages learners to take ownership of their education and actively seek out information and resources to solve problems. This self-directed learning approach cultivates lifelong learning habits, enabling individuals to stay updated with the latest developments in their field. Employers value individuals who demonstrate a proactive attitude towards learning and show the initiative to acquire new knowledge and skills independently.

Problem-Based Learning often incorporates authentic assessments, which provide individuals with opportunities to showcase their abilities in a real-world context. These assessments go beyond traditional exams and encourage individuals to apply their knowledge and skills to solve practical problems. By engaging in these assessments, individuals develop a portfolio of work that demonstrates their competency and readiness for the job market. This can greatly enhance their employability and increase their chances of securing desirable positions.

It is important to note that the results of Problem-Based Learning on the job are not limited to individuals' professional development alone. PBL has a positive impact on organizations as well. By promoting critical thinking, collaboration, and problem-solving skills, PBL contributes to the overall effectiveness and productivity of teams. Organizations that employ individuals trained in PBL methods benefit from a workforce that is better equipped to tackle challenges, drive innovation, and adapt to changing circumstances.

The True Benefactors of Problem Based Learning

The true benefactors of Problem-Based Learning (PBL) are the students themselves, as well as the educators who implement this approach. PBL offers numerous benefits that contribute to the overall growth and development of students, fostering their critical thinking skills, problem-solving abilities, and deep understanding of the subject matter.

One of the primary benefactors of PBL is the student. PBL promotes active learning and student engagement by placing them in the driver's seat of their own education. Instead of passively receiving information, students actively participate in the learning process, taking ownership of their education. Through the process of identifying and analyzing real-world problems, students are motivated to explore and understand concepts in a meaningful context. This active engagement enhances their learning experience and helps them develop a deeper understanding of the subject matter.

PBL also cultivates critical thinking skills in students. By presenting them with authentic problems, PBL encourages students to think critically and analyze information from multiple perspectives. Students are challenged to evaluate evidence, weigh different viewpoints, and make informed decisions. This process enhances their ability to think critically, assess the validity of information, and develop logical and well-reasoned arguments. These critical thinking skills are valuable not only in academic settings but also in various aspects of life, such as problem-solving in the workplace or making informed decisions as responsible citizens.

Problem-solving abilities are another area where students benefit from PBL. In PBL, students actively engage in identifying, analyzing, and solving problems, which closely reflects real-world scenarios. This approach prepares students for the challenges they may face in their future careers or daily lives. By working through complex problems, students develop problem-solving strategies, learn to think creatively, and become adept at finding innovative solutions. These problem-solving skills are transferable and can be applied to a wide range of situations beyond the classroom.

Furthermore, PBL fosters collaboration and teamwork skills. In many PBL implementations, students work in groups to solve problems collectively. This collaborative environment encourages students to communicate effectively, listen to diverse perspectives, and work together towards a common goal. They learn to respect and value different viewpoints, negotiate and compromise, and leverage the strengths of each team member. These teamwork skills are essential in professional settings, where collaboration and effective communication are often required for successful project completion.

Educators also benefit from implementing PBL. By incorporating PBL into their teaching practices, educators can witness the transformation in their students' learning experiences. PBL shifts the role of the educator from a traditional knowledge provider to a facilitator and guide. Educators have the opportunity to observe firsthand the growth of their students' critical thinking, problem-solving, and collaboration skills. They witness students becoming more independent learners, taking responsibility for their own learning, and actively engaging with the subject matter.

Moreover, PBL allows educators to create a dynamic and interactive learning environment. Instead of simply lecturing, educators can foster discussions, encourage inquiry, and provide guidance as students navigate through the problem-solving process. This active involvement helps educators gain insights into students' understanding, identify misconceptions, and provide targeted feedback and support. It also allows educators to build stronger relationships with their students, as they work together to explore and solve complex problems.

The true benefactors of Problem-Based Learning are the students and educators involved. Students benefit from active learning, critical thinking skills, problem-solving abilities, and collaborative skills developed through PBL. Educators benefit from witnessing the growth and development of their students and the creation of an interactive and engaging learning environment. PBL is a powerful educational approach that empowers students, fosters deep understanding, and prepares them for success in their academic and professional lives.

CHAPTER THREE
Cognitive and Metacognitive Processes in PBL

Problem-Based Learning (PBL) is an instructional approach that emphasizes active learning, critical thinking, and problem-solving skills. In PBL, students engage in authentic, real-world problems that require them to apply their knowledge and skills to find solutions. This chapter explores the cognitive and metacognitive processes involved in PBL and their significance in promoting effective learning. The key aspects discussed in this chapter include active learning and engagement, inquiry and critical thinking skills, self-directed learning, reflection and metacognition, and problem-solving strategies in PBL.

Active Learning and Engagement: Active learning is a fundamental component of PBL. It involves students taking an active role in their learning process, rather than passively receiving information from teachers. In PBL, students engage in problem-solving activities, collaborate with peers, and seek out resources to acquire the necessary knowledge and skills to solve the given problem. This active engagement promotes deeper understanding, retention, and transfer of knowledge. By actively participating in PBL, students become more motivated, develop a sense of ownership over their learning, and enhance their problem-solving abilities.

Engagement is another critical aspect of PBL. When students are engaged in the learning process, they are more likely to be motivated, focused, and invested in their work. PBL provides opportunities for students to explore their interests, make connections to real-world contexts, and actively participate in meaningful tasks. The engagement in PBL is facilitated through the use of authentic problems, collaborative learning environments, and opportunities for self-directed learning. These factors contribute to creating a supportive and engaging learning environment that fosters cognitive and metacognitive processes.

Inquiry and Critical Thinking Skills

PBL promotes inquiry-based learning, which involves students actively investigating problems, asking questions, and seeking solutions. Through inquiry, students develop critical thinking skills such as analysis, evaluation, and synthesis. PBL encourages students to think critically by presenting them with open-ended problems that require complex thinking and decision-making. By engaging in the process of analyzing and evaluating information, students become better at identifying relevant data, recognizing biases, and making informed judgments.

Critical thinking skills are further developed in PBL through the use of authentic assessments. Instead of relying solely on traditional exams, PBL incorporates assessments that mirror real-world scenarios, allowing students to demonstrate their ability to apply knowledge and think critically. These assessments may include presentations, group discussions, research papers, or project-based assignments. By engaging in these assessments, students gain experience in analyzing complex information, formulating arguments, and defending their ideas, enhancing their critical thinking abilities.

Self-Directed Learning

Self-directed learning is a crucial aspect of PBL. In PBL, students take responsibility for their learning by setting goals, identifying learning needs, and seeking out resources to acquire the necessary knowledge and skills. They engage in self-directed learning by conducting research, reading relevant materials, and seeking expert guidance when needed. This process fosters independent learning skills and promotes lifelong learning habits.

Self-directed learning in PBL is facilitated through scaffolding and guidance from facilitators. Facilitators provide support by structuring the learning process, providing resources, and guiding students in setting achievable goals. They encourage students to take ownership of their learning and develop skills in self-regulation, time management, and goal setting. Self-directed learning in PBL not only enhances students' knowledge and skills but also empowers them to become lifelong learners capable of adapting to new challenges and acquiring knowledge independently.

Reflection and Metacognition

Reflection and metacognition play significant roles in PBL. Reflection involves the deliberate examination and evaluation of one's own learning experiences, while metacognition refers to the awareness and understanding of one's cognitive processes. PBL provides opportunities for students to reflect on their learning process, assess their progress, and identify areas for improvement.

Reflection in PBL can take various forms, such as journaling, group discussions, or individual self-assessments. Through reflection, students gain insights into their thinking processes, identify misconceptions, and develop strategies for future learning. Metacognition, on the other hand, involves students' awareness of their thinking, learning strategies, and problem-solving approaches. By developing metacognitive skills, students become more effective learners as they can monitor their own understanding, regulate their learning strategies, and make adjustments when necessary.

Metacognition and reflection are promoted in PBL through regular debriefing sessions, where students discuss their problem-solving strategies, reflect on their learning experiences, and identify areas for improvement. Facilitators play a crucial role in guiding these discussions and helping students develop metacognitive awareness. By integrating reflection and metacognition into PBL, students become more self-aware, develop higher-order thinking skills, and become better at monitoring and regulating their own learning processes.

Problem-Solving Strategies in PBL

Problem-solving is at the core of PBL. PBL provides students with authentic, complex problems that require them to apply their knowledge and skills to find solutions. In the process of problem-solving, students engage in various strategies that help them navigate through the problem-solving process effectively.

One of the key problem-solving strategies in PBL is the use of prior knowledge. Students draw on their existing knowledge and experiences to understand the problem and make connections to relevant concepts. They also engage in research and inquiry to acquire new information and expand their knowledge base. Collaboration and teamwork are essential problem-solving strategies in PBL. Students work together in groups to brainstorm ideas, share perspectives, and collectively find solutions. Collaboration not only enhances problem-solving skills but also promotes communication, teamwork, and interpersonal skills.

Another problem-solving strategy in PBL is the iterative nature of the process. Students engage in multiple cycles of problem-solving, reflection, and revision. They analyze their initial solutions, reflect on their effectiveness, and make improvements based on feedback and new insights. This iterative process allows students to refine their problem-solving skills, develop resilience, and learn from their mistakes.

Furthermore, PBL encourages creative and innovative thinking. Students are encouraged to think outside the box, generate multiple solutions, and evaluate their viability. They explore alternative perspectives, challenge assumptions, and develop creative problem-solving approaches. By engaging in creative problem-solving, students develop their creative thinking skills and become more adaptable and resourceful in addressing real-world challenges.

Cognitive and metacognitive processes play a crucial role in the effectiveness of PBL. Active learning and engagement foster deeper understanding and promote motivation and ownership of learning. Inquiry and critical thinking skills are developed through authentic problem-solving tasks, while self-directed learning empowers students to take responsibility for their own learning. Reflection and metacognition enhance students' awareness and understanding of their learning processes, leading to more effective learning strategies.

Finally, problem-solving strategies in PBL enable students to apply their knowledge and skills to real-world problems, fostering creativity, collaboration, and resilience. By understanding and leveraging these cognitive and metacognitive processes, educators can create engaging and effective PBL experiences that promote meaningful learning and prepare students for the challenges of the 21st century.

PBL is an educational approach that emphasizes active learning, critical thinking, and problem-solving skills. It involves presenting students with real-world problems or scenarios and guiding them through the process of investigating and finding solutions. Cognitive processes involve the mental activities used to understand, analyze, and solve problems, while metacognitive processes refer to the awareness and regulation of one's own cognitive processes. In PBL, both cognitive and metacognitive processes work together to enhance learning outcomes and develop students' problem-solving abilities.

Cognitive processes in PBL encompass a range of activities that students engage in while working on a problem. These processes include problem identification, information gathering, analysis and synthesis, hypothesis generation, and evaluation of solutions. When presented with a problem, students need to identify the key issues and formulate questions to guide their investigation. This requires them to activate their prior knowledge, understand the problem context, and break down complex information into manageable parts. Information gathering involves seeking relevant resources, such as textbooks, books, or online databases, to acquire the necessary knowledge to address the problem. Students must critically evaluate the information they find, distinguishing between credible and unreliable sources.

Analysis and synthesis involve organizing and integrating the acquired information to develop a comprehensive understanding of the problem. Students engage in critical thinking to identify patterns, relationships, and potential solutions. They use their analytical skills to break down complex problems into smaller components, facilitating a more systematic approach to problem-solving. Hypothesis generation is another cognitive process where students propose potential solutions or explanations based on their understanding of the problem. They must think creatively and consider multiple perspectives to generate plausible hypotheses.

Evaluation of solutions is a critical cognitive process in PBL. Students need to assess the feasibility and effectiveness of their proposed solutions. This involves analyzing the strengths and weaknesses of each option, considering potential risks and benefits, and making informed decisions. Evaluation requires students to think critically, weigh evidence, and consider alternative perspectives. Through this process, they develop their ability to make reasoned judgments and refine their problem-solving skills.

While cognitive processes are essential in PBL, metacognitive processes play a complementary role. Metacognition involves the awareness and regulation of one's own cognitive processes. It refers to thinking about thinking, reflecting on one's knowledge, and monitoring and evaluating one's own learning. Metacognitive processes help students become more effective learners and problem solvers.

Metacognitive processes in PBL include planning, monitoring, and evaluating one's learning. When engaging in PBL, students need to plan their approach to the problem. This involves setting goals, organizing their time and resources, and developing strategies for gathering and processing information. Planning helps students stay focused and organized throughout the problem-solving process, enhancing their efficiency and effectiveness.

Monitoring is another metacognitive process that students employ in PBL. It involves keeping track of one's progress, identifying areas of confusion or gaps in understanding, and making adjustments as needed. By monitoring their own learning, students become more self-aware and can identify when they need to seek additional information or revise their strategies. Monitoring also allows students to reflect on their problem-solving process, recognizing their strengths and weaknesses, and identifying opportunities for improvement.

The final metacognitive process in PBL is evaluation. Students need to evaluate the quality and effectiveness of their problem-solving process and outcomes. They reflect on their decisions, strategies, and solutions, considering what worked well and what could be improved. Evaluation enables students to develop a deeper understanding of their own thinking processes and refine their problem-solving skills for future challenges.

To support the development of cognitive and metacognitive processes in PBL, educators play a critical role. They facilitate the learning process by guiding students through the problem-solving activities, asking probing questions, and providing feedback. Educators can help students activate their prior knowledge, encourage critical thinking, and promote metacognitive reflection. By modeling effective cognitive and metacognitive processes, educators help students develop these skills themselves.

Cognitive and metacognitive processes are fundamental to Problem-Based Learning. Cognitive processes involve problem identification, information gathering, analysis and synthesis, hypothesis generation, and evaluation of solutions. These processes enable students to understand, analyze, and solve complex problems. Metacognitive processes, on the other hand, involve planning, monitoring, and evaluating one's own learning. They enhance students' awareness of their thinking processes and enable them to regulate and improve their problem-solving skills. By integrating both cognitive and metacognitive processes, PBL promotes active learning, critical thinking, and the development of effective problem-solving abilities in students.

Once the problem is identified, students engage in information gathering. This involves seeking relevant literature, empirical studies, and other resources to acquire knowledge that can be used to address the problem. In psychology, students may consult academic journals, textbooks, or online databases to access the latest research findings and theories in the field. They critically evaluate the information they gather, considering the validity and reliability of the sources, and use this information to develop a comprehensive understanding of the problem. Analysis and synthesis are important cognitive processes in PBL.

Students break down complex information into smaller components, identify patterns and relationships, and integrate various pieces of information to develop a coherent understanding of the problem. In psychology, students may examine how different psychological theories or perspectives relate to the problem and analyze how specific variables or factors influence the outcomes. This analytical thinking helps students develop critical thinking skills and a deeper understanding of psychological concepts and theories.

Hypothesis generation is another cognitive process in PBL. Students propose potential solutions or explanations based on their understanding of the problem and the information they have gathered. In psychology, students may generate hypotheses based on psychological theories or research findings, and consider how different variables or factors may influence the outcomes. This process encourages students to think creatively and consider multiple perspectives, fostering their ability to generate innovative ideas and solutions.

Cognitive and metacognitive processes are integral to Problem-Based Learning in the field of psychology. Cognitive processes involve problem identification, information gathering, analysis and synthesis, hypothesis generation, and evaluation of solutions. These processes enable students to understand and solve complex psychological problems. Metacognitive processes, on the other hand, involve planning, monitoring, and evaluating one's own learning. They enhance students' awareness of their thinking processes and enable them to regulate and improve their problem-solving skills. By integrating both cognitive and metacognitive processes, PBL in psychology education fosters active learning, critical thinking, and the development of effective problem-solving abilities in students.

CHAPTER FOUR
Collaboration and Communication Skills

Collaboration and communication skills are essential in project-based learning (PBL) environments. PBL encourages students to work together in teams, solve problems collectively, and communicate their ideas effectively. These skills are not only important for academic success but also for success in the professional world, where teamwork and collaboration are highly valued.

In a PBL setting, students are often assigned to diverse teams with members from different backgrounds, experiences, and perspectives. This diversity brings together a range of skills and knowledge, fostering a rich learning environment. However, effective collaboration requires more than just putting individuals together; it requires the development of strong communication skills.

Effective communication involves active listening, articulating ideas clearly, and providing constructive feedback. PBL projects often involve discussions, brainstorming sessions, and presentations. By engaging in these activities, students learn to express their thoughts, actively listen to their peers, and adapt their communication styles to different audiences. These skills are transferable and can be applied to various real-world situations.

To promote collaboration and communication skills in PBL, educators can design activities that explicitly focus on these areas. For example, they can assign roles within teams, such as a facilitator or a scribe, to encourage equitable participation and ensure that everyone has a chance to contribute. Moreover, educators can provide guidelines and rubrics for effective communication, emphasizing the importance of respectful and constructive dialogue.

Teamwork and Interpersonal Relationships

Teamwork is a fundamental aspect of PBL. In a team-based PBL environment, students learn to work collectively towards a common goal, leveraging each other's strengths and collaborating to find solutions. Through teamwork, students develop interpersonal skills, such as empathy, respect, and conflict resolution, which are crucial for successful collaboration and interpersonal relationships.

PBL projects often require students to engage in discussions, make decisions together, and divide tasks among team members. These activities foster teamwork by promoting shared responsibility, mutual support, and accountability. Students learn to value the contributions of their team members, recognize individual strengths, and work towards achieving a common objective.

Interpersonal relationships play a vital role in PBL. Positive relationships within a team create a supportive and inclusive learning environment. When students feel connected to their team members, they are more likely to actively participate, share ideas, and take risks. On the other hand, conflicts or strained relationships can hinder the progress of a project and negatively impact the learning experience.

To foster teamwork and positive interpersonal relationships in PBL, educators can facilitate team-building activities at the beginning of the project. These activities can include icebreakers, trust-building exercises, and opportunities for students to get to know each other on a personal level. Additionally, educators can provide guidance on conflict resolution strategies and encourage open communication within teams.

Motivation and Engagement

Motivation and engagement are crucial for effective learning in any educational setting, and PBL is no exception. PBL projects provide students with opportunities to explore topics of interest, apply their knowledge in meaningful ways, and take ownership of their learning. This active and hands-on approach to learning often leads to increased motivation and engagement among students.

In PBL, students are presented with authentic problems or challenges that require critical thinking and problem-solving skills. They are motivated by the relevance of the task and the opportunity to make a real-world impact. PBL projects often connect to students' lives and communities, allowing them to see the purpose and value in their learning.

Moreover, PBL projects provide students with autonomy and agency over their learning. They have the freedom to make decisions, set goals, and determine the best course of action to solve the problem at hand. This sense of ownership and control empowers students and increases their motivation to succeed.

Educators can enhance motivation and engagement in PBL by designing projects that are personally meaningful and relevant to students' lives. They can provide opportunities for students to choose topics or develop their own research questions within the project's framework. Furthermore, educators can incorporate elements of gamification, such as leaderboards or rewards, to make the learning experience more engaging and enjoyable.

Student Ownership and Autonomy

Student ownership and autonomy are key components of PBL. PBL projects provide students with the freedom to explore their interests, set goals, and take responsibility for their learning. This level of ownership and autonomy fosters a sense of agency and empowers students to become active participants in their education.

In PBL, students have the opportunity to make decisions about their learning journey. They can choose the direction of their research, decide on the resources they will use, and determine how they will present their findings. This freedom allows students to develop a sense of ownership over their work and take pride in their accomplishments.

Student ownership in PBL also involves taking responsibility for the project's success. Students collaborate within their teams, share the workload, and hold each other accountable for meeting project deadlines. They learn to manage their time effectively, set priorities, and overcome obstacles. These skills are valuable not only in academic settings but also in future careers.

To promote student ownership and autonomy in PBL, educators can provide students with clear project guidelines and objectives while leaving room for flexibility and student choice. Educators can act as facilitators, guiding students through the learning process and offering support when needed. By gradually releasing control, educators empower students to become self-directed learners.

Emotional Intelligence in PBL

Emotional intelligence, the ability to recognize and manage one's own emotions and empathize with others, plays a significant role in PBL. PBL projects often involve teamwork, collaboration, and interactions with peers. Developing emotional intelligence skills can contribute to effective communication, conflict resolution, and the creation of a positive learning environment.

In PBL, students work in teams where emotions can run high due to the pressure of meeting project deadlines and the need to navigate interpersonal dynamics. Emotional intelligence allows students to recognize their own emotions and manage them in a constructive manner. It also enables them to understand and empathize with the emotions of their team members, fostering supportive and respectful interactions.

Emotional intelligence skills, such as self-awareness, self-regulation, empathy, and social skills, can be nurtured and developed within the PBL context. Educators can integrate activities that promote emotional intelligence, such as reflective journaling, role-playing scenarios, and group discussions focused on emotions and empathy. These activities encourage students to develop a deeper understanding of their own emotions and those of others.

By incorporating emotional intelligence into PBL, educators can help students develop critical social and emotional skills that are essential for success in both academic and professional settings. Students who possess emotional intelligence are better equipped to handle challenges, resolve conflicts, and collaborate effectively, leading to more positive and productive learning experiences.

The social and emotional aspects of PBL are integral to the success and effectiveness of this instructional approach. Collaboration and communication skills enable students to work effectively in teams, while teamwork and interpersonal relationships create a supportive and inclusive learning environment. Motivation and engagement are fostered through meaningful and relevant projects, and student ownership and autonomy empower students to take charge of their learning. Finally, emotional intelligence skills contribute to effective communication, conflict resolution, and the creation of a positive learning environment. By focusing on these aspects, educators can create a rich and engaging PBL experience that prepares students for success in the 21st century.

Collaboration and communication skills play a crucial role in Problem-Based Learning (PBL). PBL is an educational approach that emphasizes active learning, critical thinking, and problem-solving through collaborative efforts. In this context, effective collaboration and communication are essential for successful problem-solving and optimal learning outcomes.

Collaboration is a key component of PBL as it allows students to work together in teams to solve complex problems. Through collaboration, students can share their knowledge, skills, and perspectives, leading to a deeper understanding of the problem and more comprehensive solutions. Here's how collaboration plays a role in PBL:

1. ***Knowledge sharing:*** In collaborative PBL settings, students bring their individual expertise and experiences to the table. By working together, they can share their knowledge, insights, and diverse perspectives, leading to a richer and more comprehensive understanding of the problem. Collaborative knowledge sharing allows students to draw on each other's strengths and collectively build a deeper understanding of the subject matter.
2. ***Teamwork and division of labor***: Collaboration in PBL involves dividing tasks and responsibilities among team

members. This division of labor allows students to leverage their individual strengths and skills to contribute to the problem-solving process. Teamwork fosters cooperation, coordination, and effective utilization of resources, ensuring that the workload is distributed evenly and that each team member's contributions are valued.
3. ***Conflict resolution and negotiation:*** Collaborative PBL environments provide opportunities for students to develop conflict resolution and negotiation skills. When working in teams, disagreements and conflicts may arise due to differences in opinions or approaches. Through effective communication and problem-solving discussions, students learn to resolve conflicts, find common ground, and make decisions that benefit the team's progress. These conflict resolution and negotiation skills are valuable both within and beyond the educational setting.

Communication skills are equally important in PBL as they facilitate effective collaboration and knowledge sharing among team members. Here's how communication skills play a role in PBL:

1. *Active listening:* Active listening is crucial for effective communication in PBL. When students actively listen to their team members, they demonstrate respect and show that their contributions are valued. Active listening helps students understand different perspectives, identify key points, and ask relevant questions. It also fosters a supportive and inclusive learning environment where everyone's voice is heard and respected.
2. *Verbal and nonverbal communication:* Effective verbal and nonverbal communication skills are essential in PBL. Students need to express their ideas clearly, articulate their thoughts, and provide constructive feedback. Verbal communication allows team members to share their insights, ask questions, and engage in discussions. Nonverbal cues,

such as body language and facial expressions, also contribute to effective communication by conveying emotions, attention, and engagement.
3. *Presentation and public speaking:* In PBL, students often have to present their findings, solutions, or recommendations to their peers or instructors. Developing strong presentation and public speaking skills is important to effectively communicate their ideas, engage the audience, and convey their findings with confidence and clarity. Through these presentations, students enhance their communication skills and gain experience in delivering impactful messages.
4. *Written communication:* Written communication is another critical aspect of PBL. Students may be required to document their research findings, write reports, or collaborate on written assignments. Clear and concise written communication is essential for effectively conveying information, supporting arguments, and presenting evidence. Developing strong writing

skills enhances students' ability to articulate their thoughts and ideas effectively.
5. ***Feedback and reflection:*** Communication in PBL also involves providing and receiving feedback. Students offer constructive feedback to their peers, providing insights and suggestions for improvement. This feedback promotes critical thinking and reflection, allowing students to refine their ideas and solutions. By receiving feedback, students learn to accept and incorporate constructive criticism, fostering their personal and professional growth.

Collaboration and communication skills are integral to the success of PBL. These skills facilitate effective teamwork, knowledge sharing, conflict resolution, and the development of comprehensive problem-solving strategies. Through collaboration and effective communication, students learn to work effectively in teams, consider diverse perspectives, and present their ideas confidently. These skills are not only beneficial in the educational context but also in various personal and professional settings, where collaboration and effective communication are essential for success.

CHAPTER FIVE
PBL in Science, Technology, Engineering, and Mathematics (STEM)

Problem-Based Learning (PBL) is an instructional approach that promotes student-centered learning by engaging students in solving real-world problems. In the field of science education, PBL has gained significant attention and recognition as an effective pedagogical strategy. PBL in science education aims to enhance students' understanding of scientific concepts, develop critical thinking and problem-solving skills, and promote collaborative learning.

PBL in Science Education

In PBL, students are presented with a complex, open-ended problem or question related to a scientific concept or phenomenon. They are then required to investigate the problem, gather relevant information, and propose possible solutions or explanations based on their knowledge and scientific inquiry. Through this process, students actively construct their understanding of scientific concepts and develop inquiry skills such as data collection, analysis, and interpretation.

One of the key advantages of PBL in science education is its ability to promote authentic learning experiences. By engaging in real-world problems, students can see the relevance and applicability of scientific concepts in their lives. PBL also fosters creativity and innovation as students are encouraged to think critically and develop unique solutions to problems.

Furthermore, PBL in science education promotes collaboration and communication skills. Students often work in teams to solve the problem, which requires effective communication, cooperation, and negotiation. Collaborative problem-solving not only enhances students' interpersonal skills but also prepares them for future careers in science and related fields where teamwork is crucial.

To implement PBL effectively in science education, teachers play a crucial role in guiding and facilitating the learning process.

They act as coaches or mentors, providing guidance and support while allowing students to take ownership of their learning. Teachers can design authentic problems, facilitate discussions, and provide feedback to help students refine their understanding and solutions.

PBL in Technology Education

PBL is also widely used in technology education to promote hands-on learning and foster problem-solving skills in relation to technological concepts and applications. Technology education aims to equip students with the knowledge and skills to understand, use, and create technology effectively and responsibly.

In PBL for technology education, students are presented with real-world challenges that require them to apply technological knowledge and skills to develop innovative solutions. These challenges can range from designing and building prototypes to addressing technological issues or improving existing systems. By engaging in such projects, students gain practical experience and a deeper understanding of how technology impacts various aspects of their lives.

PBL in technology education helps students develop critical thinking, creativity, and problem-solving skills. They learn to identify problems, generate ideas, and design solutions by considering constraints, evaluating alternatives, and making informed decisions. PBL also promotes interdisciplinary learning, as students often need to integrate knowledge and skills from different areas, such as engineering, mathematics, and science, to address technological challenges effectively.

Moreover, PBL in technology education nurtures students' innovation and entrepreneurial mindset. By engaging in hands-on projects, students have the opportunity to create prototypes, test their ideas, and refine their designs based on feedback and evaluation. They develop resilience, adaptability, and an understanding of the iterative nature of technological innovation.

Teachers in technology education play the role of facilitators, guiding students through the PBL process. They provide the necessary resources, tools, and technical expertise to support students' learning. Teachers also encourage reflection and metacognition, helping students understand their learning processes and make connections between theoretical concepts and practical applications.

PBL in Engineering Education

Engineering education focuses on developing students' understanding of engineering principles and practices. PBL has been widely adopted in engineering education due to its effectiveness in promoting problem-solving, critical thinking, and teamwork skills, which are essential for engineering professionals.

PBL in engineering education involves presenting students with authentic engineering challenges or design problems. These challenges can range from designing a bridge or a sustainable energy system to developing a new product or improving an existing technology. Students work in teams to analyze the problem, conduct research, brainstorm ideas, and design and test solutions. Through this process, they develop engineering skills such as analysis, synthesis, evaluation, and communication.

One of the key benefits of PBL in engineering education is its ability to provide students with hands-on experiences. By engaging in real-world engineering challenges, students gain practical knowledge and skills that are directly applicable to their future careers. They learn to apply scientific principles, mathematical concepts, and engineering design processes to solve complex problems.

PBL in engineering education also fosters creativity and innovation. Students are encouraged to think outside the box, explore multiple solutions, and embrace failure as an opportunity for learning and improvement. They develop the ability to identify constraints, consider trade-offs, and make informed decisions in the design and implementation of engineering projects.

Collaboration and communication skills are integral to PBL in engineering education. Students work in teams, simulating the collaborative nature of engineering projects in professional settings. They learn to effectively communicate their ideas, listen to others' perspectives, and work towards a common goal. These skills are essential for successful engineering practice, as engineers often work in multidisciplinary teams to tackle complex problems.

Teachers in engineering education play a vital role in facilitating PBL. They provide guidance and mentorship, ensuring that students have access to the necessary resources and tools. Teachers also encourage reflection on the engineering design process, helping students analyze their experiences, identify areas for improvement, and develop a deep understanding of engineering principles and practices.

PBL in Mathematics Education

PBL can also be effectively applied in mathematics education to enhance students' understanding of mathematical concepts and promote problem-solving and critical thinking skills. Traditional mathematics instruction often focuses on procedural fluency, but PBL in mathematics education shifts the emphasis to conceptual understanding and the application of mathematical knowledge in real-world contexts.

In PBL for mathematics education, students are presented with mathematical problems or scenarios that require them to apply mathematical concepts and techniques to solve them. These problems can be related to various real-life situations, such as financial planning, data analysis, or optimization. Students are encouraged to explore multiple solution strategies, make connections between different mathematical ideas, and communicate their reasoning effectively.

Through PBL, students develop a deeper understanding of mathematical concepts and their applications. They see the relevance of mathematics in their daily lives and understand how mathematical thinking can be used to solve practical problems. PBL also helps students develop critical thinking skills by challenging them to analyze problems, make conjectures, test hypotheses, and evaluate the reasonableness of their solutions.

Collaboration and communication skills are essential components of PBL in mathematics education. Students often work in teams to solve mathematical problems, sharing their strategies, discussing alternative approaches, and justifying their reasoning. By engaging in collaborative problem-solving, students develop effective communication skills, learn from their peers, and appreciate multiple perspectives.

PBL in mathematics education also promotes the integration of technology. Students can utilize various technological tools, such as graphing calculators, spreadsheets, and mathematical software, to explore, visualize, and analyze mathematical concepts. Technology enhances students' mathematical reasoning and enables them to tackle complex problems that may not be feasible using traditional paper-and-pencil methods.

Teachers in mathematics education serve as facilitators in PBL, guiding students through the problem-solving process. They help students make connections between mathematical concepts and real-world applications, provide support and scaffolding when needed, and promote mathematical discourse in the classroom. Teachers also encourage reflection and metacognition, helping students develop a deep understanding of mathematical principles and problem-solving strategies.

Integration of STEM Disciplines in PBL

Integrating science, technology, engineering, and mathematics (STEM) disciplines in PBL can create rich and authentic learning experiences that reflect the interdisciplinary nature of real-world challenges. The integration of STEM in PBL allows students to see the connections between these disciplines and understand how they work together to solve complex problems.

In STEM-focused PBL, students are presented with problems or projects that require the integration of knowledge and skills from multiple STEM disciplines. For example, students may be tasked with designing and constructing a model solar-powered vehicle. To complete this project successfully, they need to apply scientific principles to understand the conversion of solar energy, use engineering design processes to develop a functional and efficient vehicle, apply mathematical concepts for measurement and optimization, and utilize technology for data collection and analysis.

The integration of STEM disciplines in PBL promotes a holistic understanding of real-world problems. It encourages students to approach challenges from multiple perspectives, fostering a more comprehensive and creative problem-solving process. Students learn to think critically, make connections between different STEM concepts, and apply their knowledge and skills in an interdisciplinary manner.

Collaboration and teamwork play a crucial role in integrated STEM PBL. Students from different STEM disciplines work together, bringing their unique expertise and perspectives to the problem-solving process. This collaborative environment mirrors the interdisciplinary nature of STEM professions, where professionals with diverse backgrounds collaborate to address complex challenges.

Integrated STEM PBL also emphasizes the development of 21st-century skills. Students engage in authentic problem-solving experiences that require critical thinking, creativity, communication, and collaboration. They learn to adapt to different roles within a team, effectively communicate their ideas, and appreciate the value of diverse perspectives and expertise.

Teachers in integrated STEM PBL act as facilitators, guiding students through the interdisciplinary problem-solving process. They foster a supportive and inclusive learning environment, encourage collaboration and communication, and provide guidance in navigating the complexities of integrated

STEM projects. Teachers also promote reflection and metacognition, helping students make connections between different STEM concepts and develop a deep understanding of the interdisciplinary nature of STEM disciplines.

Problem-Based Learning (PBL) is an instructional methodology that emphasizes active learning through the exploration of real-world problems. It has gained significant recognition as an effective approach in Science, Technology, Engineering, and Mathematics (STEM) education. This book aims to discuss the importance of PBL in STEM disciplines, highlighting its benefits in fostering critical thinking, problem-solving skills, collaboration, and engagement among learners.

Enhancing Critical Thinking and Problem-Solving Skills: One of the fundamental goals of STEM education is to cultivate critical thinking and problem-solving skills in students. PBL provides a practical platform for learners to develop these skills by presenting them with authentic, complex problems. Through the process of PBL, students are challenged to analyze the problem, gather relevant information, propose hypotheses, and devise innovative solutions. This hands-on approach encourages students to think critically, apply their knowledge, and develop a deeper understanding of STEM concepts.

Promoting Collaboration and Teamwork: In the professional world, STEM fields often require collaboration and teamwork to tackle complex challenges. PBL encourages students to work in teams, simulating real-world scenarios and fostering effective communication, negotiation, and cooperation. Collaborative problem-solving in PBL environments exposes students to diverse perspectives and encourages them to draw upon each other's strengths, resulting in comprehensive solutions that consider multiple viewpoints. These teamwork experiences prepare students for future STEM careers, where collaboration is essential for success.

Engagement and Active Learning: Traditional didactic teaching methods often struggle to keep students engaged and motivated. PBL addresses this challenge by placing students at the center of the learning process, making it inherently student-driven and interactive. By actively engaging in problem-solving, students become more invested in their learning, resulting in increased motivation and deeper comprehension. PBL also taps into students' natural curiosity by presenting them with real-world problems, sparking their interest and enthusiasm for STEM subjects.

Connecting Theory with Practice: PBL bridges the gap between theoretical concepts and their practical applications, aligning with the core principles of STEM education. By engaging in hands-on problem-solving activities, students can directly observe the relevance and applicability of STEM knowledge. PBL provides opportunities for students to see the direct impact of their learning in real-world contexts, reinforcing the importance of STEM disciplines and inspiring them to pursue further exploration in these fields.

Developing Lifelong Learners: STEM fields are dynamic and rapidly evolving, requiring professionals to continuously adapt and update their knowledge and skills. PBL nurtures a growth mindset and encourages students to become lifelong learners. Through PBL, students develop the ability to seek out and evaluate information, learn independently, and adapt their problem-solving strategies as new challenges arise. By cultivating these skills, PBL equips students with the tools necessary to thrive in an ever-changing STEM landscape.

Fostering Creativity and Innovation: PBL promotes creativity and innovation by providing an environment that encourages students to think outside the box. When faced with open-ended problems, students are challenged to explore unconventional approaches and generate novel solutions. PBL nurtures creativity by empowering students to take risks, experiment with different ideas, and learn from both successes and failures. By fostering these qualities, PBL prepares students to become innovative problem solvers, a vital attribute in STEM disciplines.

Addressing Real-World Challenges: STEM disciplines are closely intertwined with addressing real-world challenges and finding sustainable solutions. PBL aligns with this practical aspect by presenting students with authentic problems that mirror the challenges faced by professionals in STEM fields. By immersing students in these scenarios, PBL instills a sense of purpose and relevance in their learning, empowering them to make meaningful contributions to society by leveraging their STEM knowledge and skills.

Authentic Problem Scenarios: One of the key strengths of PBL is its ability to simulate real-world scenarios. PBL tasks are designed to mirror the challenges faced by professionals in a given field, be it in science, technology, engineering, mathematics, or other disciplines. By working on authentic problems, students gain a deeper understanding of the complexity and interconnectedness of real-world challenges. This exposure prepares them to address similar issues when they transition to professional settings.

Interdisciplinary Approach: Real-world challenges often require interdisciplinary solutions, as they rarely fit within the confines of a single field. PBL encourages students to draw upon knowledge and skills from multiple disciplines to solve complex problems. By working collaboratively with peers from different backgrounds, students gain a broader perspective and learn to appreciate diverse approaches to problem-solving. This interdisciplinary approach not only enhances the quality of solutions but also cultivates a holistic understanding of real-world challenges.

Application of Knowledge: Traditional teaching methods often focus on memorization and regurgitation of information. In contrast, PBL emphasizes the application of knowledge in practical contexts. Students are required to analyze, synthesize, and evaluate information in order to develop innovative solutions to real-world problems. This application-based learning not only strengthens students' grasp of fundamental concepts but also equips them with the skills needed to adapt their knowledge to new and unfamiliar situations.

Critical Thinking and Problem-Solving Skills: Real-world challenges are rarely straightforward and often require creative problem-solving approaches. PBL promotes critical thinking by challenging students to analyze problems from multiple angles, consider different perspectives, and identify underlying issues. Through the iterative process of PBL, students learn to formulate hypotheses, gather evidence, and evaluate possible solutions. This analytical and problem-solving mindset nurtured by PBL is invaluable for addressing complex challenges in various fields.

Collaboration and Communication: Many real-world challenges demand collaborative efforts to find comprehensive solutions. PBL fosters collaboration by requiring students to work in teams. Through effective communication and negotiation, students learn to leverage their collective knowledge and skills. Collaboration in PBL environments encourages the exchange of ideas, promotes constructive feedback, and cultivates a sense of shared responsibility. These collaborative experiences prepare students for the teamwork required in professional settings.

Risk-Taking and Resilience: Real-world challenges often involve uncertainty and risk. PBL provides students with a safe space to take risks, experiment with different approaches, and learn from failures. By encouraging students to embrace failure as a stepping stone to success, PBL nurtures resilience and a growth mindset. This resilience is essential for tackling real-world challenges, as it empowers students to persevere through setbacks and continue seeking innovative solutions.

Empowering Students as Agents of Change: PBL instills a sense of purpose and agency in students by engaging them in real-world challenges. By addressing pressing issues, students recognize the potential impact of their solutions on society. PBL empowers students to become agents of change, encouraging them to apply their knowledge and skills to make a positive difference in the world. This sense of purpose inspires students to become lifelong learners and motivates them to pursue careers in fields where they can contribute to solving real-world challenges.

Problem-Based Learning (PBL) plays a decisive function in STEM education, as it promotes critical thinking, problem-solving skills, collaboration, engagement, and creativity. By integrating PBL into the curriculum, educators can create an environment that mirrors the real-world challenges of STEM professionals. The benefits of PBL extend beyond the classroom, equipping students with the skills necessary for success in STEM careers and fostering a lifelong love of learning. PBL's ability to connect theory with practice, address real-world challenges, and promote interdisciplinary collaboration makes it an indispensable tool in preparing the next generation of STEM leaders.

PBL in science, technology, engineering, and mathematics (STEM) education offers numerous benefits for students' learning and development. It promotes authentic learning experiences, enhances understanding of disciplinary concepts, and fosters critical thinking, problem-solving, collaboration, and communication skills. By integrating STEM disciplines in PBL, students are exposed to the interdisciplinary nature of real-world challenges, preparing them for future careers and enabling them to make meaningful contributions to society. Teachers play a vital role in facilitating PBL, providing guidance and support, and creating a conducive environment for student-centered and inquiry-based learning. With the continued implementation of PBL in STEM education, students can develop the skills and knowledge necessary to tackle the complex challenges of the 21st century.

CHAPTER SIX
Technology and Problem-Based Learning

In today's digital age, technology plays a crucial role in transforming various aspects of education, including project-based learning (PBL). This chapter explores the integration of digital tools and resources in PBL, the emergence of online and virtual PBL environments, the adoption of blended approaches, and the challenges and opportunities associated with technology-enhanced PBL.

Digital Tools and Resources for PBL

Digital tools and resources have revolutionized the way educators and students engage in PBL. These tools provide opportunities for collaboration, research, organization, and presentation, enhancing the overall learning experience. Various types of digital tools are available to support different stages of the PBL process. For example, tools like Google Docs and Microsoft Office 365 facilitate collaborative writing and document sharing, allowing students to work together on project deliverables. Online databases and research platforms enable students to access a wealth of information and engage in meaningful inquiry. Additionally, multimedia creation tools like video editors and graphic design software empower students to express their ideas creatively and present their projects in visually appealing ways.

Online and Virtual PBL Environments

The rise of online and virtual learning environments has opened up new possibilities for PBL. These environments enable students to collaborate and engage in project work regardless of their physical location. Online PBL platforms provide a centralized space for project management, communication, and resource sharing. Students can access project materials, submit assignments, and communicate with their peers and teachers asynchronously. Virtual PBL environments, on the other hand, leverage virtual reality (VR) and augmented reality (AR) technologies to create immersive learning experiences. Students can explore virtual simulations, conduct experiments, and interact with virtual objects, enhancing their understanding of complex concepts and real-world applications.

Blended Approaches to PBL

Blended learning, which combines face-to-face instruction with online components, has gained popularity in recent years. This approach can be effectively applied to PBL, allowing for a balance between in-person collaboration and digital engagement. In a blended PBL model, students may work on projects both in the classroom and through online platforms. Face-to-face meetings provide opportunities for brainstorming, team building, and hands-on activities, while online components offer flexibility, independent research, and virtual collaboration. Blended PBL also allows educators to leverage the strengths of both traditional and digital resources, catering to different learning styles and preferences.

Challenges and Opportunities in Technology-Enhanced PBL

While technology enhances PBL in numerous ways, it also presents certain challenges. One key challenge is access to technology and reliable internet connectivity, as not all students have equal access to devices or stable internet connections. This digital divide can create disparities in PBL experiences and limit the opportunities for some students. Additionally, integrating technology into PBL requires careful planning and professional development for educators to ensure effective implementation. Teachers need support and training to understand how to leverage digital tools and resources optimally and align them with learning objectives.

However, despite these challenges, technology also brings forth numerous opportunities for PBL. It enables authentic and real-world connections by facilitating collaboration with experts, professionals, and other students worldwide. Technology also promotes student agency and autonomy by providing opportunities for self-directed learning and exploration. Furthermore, it enhances the visibility and dissemination of student work, as projects can be shared online and reach a global audience.

Digital tools and resources offer new avenues for collaboration, research, and presentation, enriching the PBL experience. Online and virtual environments extend the possibilities of PBL, enabling asynchronous collaboration and immersive learning. Blended approaches combine in-person and online elements, providing a flexible and comprehensive learning experience. While challenges such as access and implementation exist, the opportunities presented by technology in PBL are vast, fostering authentic connections, student agency, and global visibility for student work. Let's explore the relationship between technology and Problem-Based Learning, highlighting the various ways in which technology can be used to support and enhance PBL, along with relevant examples.

Online Collaboration Tools

Technology provides a range of online collaboration tools that facilitate communication and collaboration among students, even when they are physically distant. Platforms such as Google Docs, Microsoft Teams, and Slack enable students to work together in real-time, share documents, brainstorm ideas, and provide feedback to each other. These tools can be particularly beneficial for PBL, as students can collaborate on problem-solving tasks, share their perspectives, and collectively develop solutions.

For example, in a science class, students can use Google Docs to collaboratively analyze experimental data, discuss observations, and propose hypotheses to solve a scientific problem. They can work on the same document simultaneously, view each other's contributions, and engage in meaningful discussions.

Multimedia Resources

Technology provides access to a wealth of multimedia resources, including videos, simulations, interactive websites, and virtual reality applications. These resources can be integrated into PBL activities to provide students with authentic and engaging learning experiences. For instance, students can watch instructional videos or interactive simulations that demonstrate real-world applications of the concepts they are learning, allowing them to connect theory with practice.

In a mathematics class, students can use virtual manipulatives and interactive simulations to understand geometric concepts, explore patterns, and solve mathematical problems. These resources make learning more interactive and visual, helping students grasp abstract concepts more effectively.

Online Research and Information Literacy

Technology enables students to conduct online research to gather information, analyze data, and explore different perspectives on a given problem. Search engines, online databases, and academic journals provide a vast amount of information that students can access to deepen their understanding and develop well-informed solutions.

For instance, in a history class, students can use online archives, primary sources, and scholarly books to investigate historical events or analyze conflicting accounts of the past. They can critically evaluate sources, consider bias, and develop evidence-based arguments as part of their problem-solving process.

Digital Portfolios and Reflection

Technology allows students to create digital portfolios to document their learning journey throughout the PBL process. Digital portfolios can include artifacts such as research papers, multimedia presentations, videos, and reflective journals. These portfolios provide a platform for students to showcase their achievements, reflect on their learning, and assess their growth over time.

For example, in a language arts class, students can create digital portfolios to showcase their written work, presentations, and recordings of oral presentations. They can also include reflections on their learning process, identifying strengths, areas for improvement, and lessons learned. Digital portfolios provide a means for students to demonstrate their understanding and self-assessment skills.

Online Discussion Forums and Blogs

Technology facilitates online discussion forums and blogs where students can engage in asynchronous discussions, share ideas, and reflect on their learning. These platforms encourage active participation, critical thinking, and the development of persuasive arguments. Students can pose questions, respond to their peers' ideas, and engage in meaningful dialogues.

For instance, in a social studies class, students can participate in an online forum to discuss current events, analyze different perspectives, and propose solutions to societal issues. They can debate, challenge assumptions, and collectively generate innovative ideas.

Mobile Devices and Apps

Technology has made mobile devices and educational apps readily available, providing opportunities for anytime, anywhere learning. Students can use smartphones or tablets to access educational apps that support PBL, enabling them to engage with content and complete tasks even outside the traditional classroom setting.

For example, in a biology class, students can use an app that allows them to scan and identify different species of plants or animals. They can explore their surroundings, collect data, and analyze biodiversity patterns. Mobile devices and apps facilitate hands-on learning experiences, making PBL more accessible and engaging.

Data Visualization Tools

Technology offers a wide range of data visualization tools that enable students to represent and analyze data effectively. These tools allow students to create charts, graphs, and infographics that help them identify patterns, draw conclusions, and communicate their findings visually. In a science class, students can use data visualization tools to analyze scientific data and represent their experimental results graphically. They can identify trends, make comparisons, and draw evidence-based conclusions. Data visualization tools enhance students' data analysis skills and promote effective communication of scientific findings.

Problem-Based Learning Application in Industries

When combined with technology, PBL becomes even more powerful, offering innovative solutions and enhancing learning experiences across different industries. This book explores the application of technology and PBL in ten diverse industries, highlighting the benefits and examples of their integration.

Healthcare Industry

Technology has transformed the healthcare industry, and PBL can be effectively used to train healthcare professionals. For example, medical students can use virtual patient simulators to diagnose and treat various conditions. These simulators provide realistic scenarios, allowing students to apply their knowledge and skills in a safe environment.

Environmental Conservation

PBL combined with technology can address environmental challenges. Students can collaborate on projects to develop innovative solutions for issues such as pollution, deforestation, and climate change. They can use sensor technology to monitor environmental parameters, create models to simulate ecosystems, and propose sustainable practices.

Engineering and Construction

In the engineering and construction industry, PBL can be used to solve complex problems. Students can work on projects that involve designing structures, optimizing energy efficiency, or developing innovative materials. Technology tools like computer-aided design (CAD) software, Building Information Modeling (BIM), and virtual reality can enhance the design and construction process.

Business and Entrepreneurship

PBL combined with technology can foster critical thinking and entrepreneurial skills. Students can engage in projects that involve creating business plans, analyzing market trends, and developing innovative solutions. Technology tools like data analytics software, e-commerce platforms, and digital marketing tools can support their entrepreneurial endeavors.

Education and E-Learning

Technology has revolutionized the education industry, and PBL can enhance e-learning experiences. Students can engage in collaborative projects that involve creating educational content, designing online courses, or developing educational games. They can use learning management systems, video conferencing tools, and online collaboration platforms to work together and deliver interactive learning experiences.

Manufacturing and Robotics

PBL can be applied in the manufacturing industry to solve production challenges. Students can work on projects that involve optimizing manufacturing processes, improving quality control, or developing automated systems. They can use robotics, programmable logic controllers (PLCs), and simulation software to design and test manufacturing solutions.

Agriculture and Food Production

PBL combined with technology can address issues in agriculture and food production. Students can engage in projects that focus on sustainable farming practices, crop optimization, or food safety. They can use remote sensing technology, Internet of Things (IoT) devices, and data analytics to monitor and manage agricultural systems.

Renewable Energy

PBL can play a vital role in the renewable energy industry. Students can work on projects that involve designing and implementing renewable energy systems, such as solar panels or wind turbines. They can use simulation software, energy monitoring tools, and data analysis to optimize energy generation and consumption.

Transportation and Logistics

PBL combined with technology can improve transportation and logistics operations. Students can engage in projects that aim to optimize supply chain management, reduce transportation costs, or improve logistics efficiency. They can use transportation simulation software, route optimization algorithms, and tracking systems to develop innovative solutions.

Entertainment and Media

PBL can be applied in the entertainment and media industry to create engaging content. Students can work on projects that involve developing multimedia productions, designing interactive experiences, or analyzing audience preferences. They can use video editing software, animation tools, and data analytics to create compelling content and understand consumer behavior.

Technology and Problem-Based Learning have the potential to revolutionize various industries, providing innovative solutions to complex problems. The healthcare industry can benefit from virtual patient simulators, while environmental conservation can be advanced through sensor technology. Engineering. Technology has revolutionized the implementation of Problem-Based Learning by providing various tools and resources that support student engagement, collaboration, critical thinking, and problem-solving skills.

Online collaboration tools, multimedia resources, online research, digital portfolios, online discussion forums, mobile devices and apps, and data visualization tools are just a few examples of how technology can be integrated into PBL. As technology continues to advance, it is crucial for educators to leverage these tools effectively to create authentic and meaningful learning experiences for students, fostering their growth as problem solvers and critical thinkers in the digital age.

CHAPTER SEVEN
Assessment and Evaluation in PBL

In Project-Based Learning (PBL), assessment and evaluation play a crucial role in determining the effectiveness of the learning experience and measuring students' understanding and growth. Unlike traditional assessment methods that focus solely on testing knowledge acquisition, PBL emphasizes authentic assessment, collaborative skills, and individual contributions. This chapter explores various aspects of assessment and evaluation in PBL, including authentic assessment methods, rubrics and criteria for PBL, assessing collaborative skills and individual contributions, feedback and reflection on learning, and evaluating the impact of PBL.

Authentic Assessment Methods

Authentic assessment methods in PBL are designed to reflect real-world contexts and tasks, enabling students to apply their knowledge and skills in meaningful ways. These assessments go beyond simple recall or regurgitation of information and require students to demonstrate their understanding through practical application and problem-solving. Some common authentic assessment methods in PBL include:

1. ***Presentations:*** Students present their projects to an audience, showcasing their research, problem-solving strategies, and solutions. Presentations can be done in various formats, such as oral presentations, multimedia presentations, or poster presentations.
2. ***Exhibitions:*** Similar to presentations, exhibitions involve displaying students' work and providing explanations to visitors. Exhibitions often take the form of a gallery walk, where students rotate among different project stations and engage in discussions about their work.
3. ***Portfolios:*** Portfolios are collections of students' work that demonstrate their progress and learning throughout the project. Portfolios can include written reflections, project artifacts, research notes, and other evidence of learning.

4. Performance-based assessments: These assessments require students to demonstrate their skills through hands-on tasks or simulations. For example, in a science project, students might design and conduct experiments or build prototypes to test their hypotheses.
5. *Interviews*: Interviews can be conducted to assess students' understanding, problem-solving approaches, and reflections on their learning. Interviews can be one-on-one or conducted in groups, allowing students to articulate their thoughts and showcase their learning process.

The use of authentic assessment methods in PBL promotes deeper learning, as students are actively engaged in applying their knowledge and skills to real-world problems and scenarios.

Rubrics and Criteria for PBL

Rubrics and criteria provide clear guidelines and expectations for student performance in PBL. They help assess student work consistently and fairly by outlining the key components and characteristics of quality work. Rubrics and criteria should be developed collaboratively with students to ensure their understanding and ownership of the assessment process. Some *Authenticity:* key considerations when designing rubrics and criteria for PBL include:

1. *Clear expectations:* Rubrics should clearly communicate the expectations for each aspect of the project. This includes criteria for content knowledge, problem-solving skills, communication skills, collaboration, and creativity.
2. *Levels of performance*: Rubrics often include different levels of performance (e.g., novice, proficient, advanced) to provide a range of assessment outcomes. Each level should be clearly defined to avoid ambiguity and support consistent evaluation. Rubrics should align with authentic assessment methods and reflect the real-world context of the project. They should assess skills and competencies that are relevant and valuable beyond the classroom.

3. ***Feedback-oriented:*** Rubrics should facilitate constructive feedback by highlighting areas of strength and areas for improvement. They should guide students in understanding how they can enhance their work and provide a roadmap for growth.

Rubrics and criteria serve as valuable tools for both students and teachers, ensuring transparency and fairness in the assessment process and promoting student engagement and self-reflection.

Assessing Collaborative Skills and Individual Contributions

Collaboration is a fundamental aspect of PBL, and assessing collaborative skills and individual contributions is essential to foster effective teamwork and accountability. While assessing collaboration can be challenging, there are several strategies and tools that can be employed:

1. ***Peer assessment:*** Peer assessment allows students to evaluate their peers' contributions and teamwork. This can be

done through structured forms or rubrics that focus on individual and group contributions, communication, reliability, and cooperation. Peer assessment encourages students to reflect on their own contributions and helps develop a sense of shared responsibility.

2. ***Team contracts:*** Team contracts are agreements created by the members of a group that outline their roles, responsibilities, and expectations. Team contracts can serve as a reference point for assessing individual contributions by comparing them against the agreed-upon roles and responsibilities.

3. ***Observations and reflections:*** Teachers can observe and provide feedback on group interactions during project work. This can be done through classroom observations, group discussions, or structured reflection activities. Observations and reflections help assess individual participation, collaboration skills, and contributions to the team.

4. ***Individual reflections:*** Individual reflections provide students with an

opportunity to articulate their contributions to the project and their learning experience. Reflection prompts can focus on aspects such as personal growth, challenges faced, and lessons learned through collaboration. Individual reflections can be used to gauge students' understanding of their role in the project and their ability to work effectively within a team.

Assessing collaborative skills and individual contributions in PBL promotes accountability, communication, and teamwork, skills that are highly valued in professional settings.

Feedback and Reflection on Learning

Feedback and reflection are integral components of the PBL process, supporting students' growth and improvement. Effective feedback and reflection practices in PBL include:

1. ***Ongoing formative feedback:*** Providing timely and specific feedback throughout the project helps students make continuous progress. Teachers can offer

feedback during project work sessions, discussions, and individual conferences. Feedback should focus on both content knowledge and the development of critical thinking, problem-solving, and communication skills.
2. *Self-assessment:* Encouraging students to assess their own work fosters metacognitive skills and self-regulation. Self-assessments activities can include checklists, rubrics, and reflection prompts that guide students in evaluating their progress, identifying strengths and weaknesses, and setting goals for improvement.
3. *Peer feedback:* Peer feedback allows students to learn from each other and develop their critical thinking and communication skills. Structured peer feedback activities can include protocols or guidelines for providing constructive feedback. Students can exchange drafts, project artifacts, or presentations and provide feedback based on the established criteria.
4. *Reflective journals:* Reflective journals provide a space for students to document

their thoughts, observations, and reflections throughout the project. Teachers can provide guiding prompts or questions to facilitate deeper reflection. Reflective journals help students internalize their learning experiences, connect concepts, and gain insights into their learning process.

Feedback and reflection in PBL support students in understanding their strengths and areas for improvement, fostering a growth mindset and promoting continuous learning.

Evaluating the Impact of PBL

Evaluating the impact of PBL involves assessing the effectiveness of the instructional approach, the learning outcomes achieved, and the overall benefits to students. Some strategies for evaluating the impact of PBL include:

1. ***Pre and post-assessment:*** Conducting pre- and post-assessments allows for the comparison of students' knowledge and skills before and after engaging in a PBL experience. This helps measure the growth in content knowledge and the

development of critical thinking, problem-solving, and other targeted skills.
2. ***Surveys and questionnaires:*** Surveys and questionnaires can be administered to students, teachers, and parents to gather feedback on the effectiveness of PBL. These tools can capture perceptions, attitudes, and experiences related to the learning process, engagement, collaboration, and the development of 21st-century skills.
3. ***Interviews and focus groups:*** Conducting interviews and focus groups with students, teachers, and other stakeholders provides qualitative data on their experiences with PBL. These methods allow for in-depth exploration of the benefits, challenges, and areas for improvement related to PBL implementation.
4. ***Long-term outcomes:*** Evaluating the long-term impact of PBL involves examining how students transfer their learning to new contexts, careers, or further education. Tracking alumni and conducting follow-up surveys or

interviews can provide insights into the lasting effects of PBL on students' academic, personal, and professional development.

Evaluating the impact of PBL helps educators refine their instructional practices, identify areas for improvement, and advocate for the benefits of PBL to stakeholders. Assessment and evaluation in PBL go beyond traditional testing methods and focus on authentic assessment, collaborative skills, and individual contributions. Authentic assessment methods reflect real-world tasks and contexts, allowing students to apply their knowledge and skills meaningfully. Rubrics and criteria provide guidelines and expectations for student performance, ensuring transparency and consistency in assessment. Assessing collaborative skills and individual contributions fosters effective teamwork and accountability. Feedback and reflection support students' growth and improvement throughout the PBL process. Lastly, evaluating the impact of PBL helps measure the effectiveness of the instructional approach and the learning outcomes achieved, providing valuable insights for continuous improvement and advocacy.

When and Where Assessment Evaluation Takes Place

Assessment and evaluation play crucial roles in PBL, as they provide feedback to students and educators about the effectiveness of the learning process. In this book, we will explore when and where assessment and evaluation take place in the context of Problem-Based Learning.

Assessment in PBL takes place at different stages of the learning process. Let's discuss these stages in detail:

1. *Initial Assessment:* Before engaging in problem-solving, students need to possess a certain level of knowledge and skills relevant to the problem at hand. Therefore, an initial assessment is often conducted to determine students' prior knowledge and identify any gaps that need to be addressed. This assessment may take the form of a pre-test or a

diagnostic test. It helps instructors understand the starting point of each student and tailor the learning experience accordingly.

2. ***Formative Assessment:*** Formative assessment occurs throughout the PBL process and is designed to provide ongoing feedback to students. It helps them track their progress, identify areas for improvement, and make adjustments to their learning strategies. Formative assessments in PBL can include peer evaluations, self-assessments, and instructor feedback during group discussions or individual consultations. These assessments foster reflection, critical thinking, and self-regulated learning.

3. ***Summative Assessment:*** Summative assessment in PBL typically occurs at the end of a learning cycle or unit. It aims to evaluate students' overall understanding of the problem, their ability to apply knowledge and skills, and the quality of their solutions. Summative assessments

may include written reports, presentations, simulations, or even practical demonstrations. These assessments provide a holistic view of students' learning outcomes and are often used for grading or certification purposes.

Assessment in PBL takes place in various settings and contexts. Let's explore the different locations where assessment occurs in PBL:

1. ***Classroom:*** The classroom is the primary setting where PBL takes place. It serves as the hub for problem-solving discussions, group work, and interactions between students and instructors. In this setting, formative assessment methods like observation, questioning, and group presentations are commonly used. These methods allow instructors to monitor student progress, facilitate discussions, and provide timely feedback.

2. ***Simulation Laboratories:*** Some PBL scenarios may require students to engage in hands-on activities or simulations. Simulation laboratories provide an environment where students can apply their theoretical knowledge to practical situations. In these labs, students' performance can be assessed through direct observation, structured checklists, or video recordings. This type of assessment allows instructors to evaluate students' ability to transfer knowledge and skills from theory to practice.

3. ***Clinical Settings:*** PBL is often used in professional programs such as medical, nursing, or veterinary education. In these programs, students are expected to apply their problem-solving skills in real clinical settings. Assessment in clinical settings can involve direct observation of students' interactions with patients, written reflections, case presentations, or standardized patient encounters. Assessments in clinical settings provide valuable feedback on students' ability to

apply knowledge, make decisions, and communicate effectively.

4. **Online Platforms:** With the advent of technology, PBL can also be conducted in online or blended learning environments. Online platforms offer various assessment tools such as quizzes, discussion boards, and multimedia presentations. These platforms allow students to collaborate remotely and receive immediate feedback on their progress. Online assessments can be both formative and summative, providing instructors with data on student performance and enabling personalized instruction.

Assessment and evaluation are integral components of Problem-Based Learning. They serve to guide students' learning, provide feedback, and measure the attainment of learning outcomes. Assessment occurs at different stages of the PBL process, including initial assessment, formative assessment, and summative assessment. Furthermore, assessment in PBL takes place in various locations, such as the classroom, simulation laboratories, clinical settings, and online platforms. The diverse nature of assessment in PBL ensures that students' progress and performance are effectively evaluated in both theoretical and practical contexts. By integrating assessment and evaluation effectively, educators can enhance the overall learning experience and promote student success in Problem-Based Learning.

Assessment in PBL involves the systematic gathering and interpretation of information about students' learning progress, performance, and achievements. It aims to determine the extent to which students have met the learning outcomes and competencies set for a PBL curriculum. Assessment methods in PBL can vary and may include individual and group assessments, as well as formative and summative assessments.

Feedback and Monitoring: Assessment provides timely feedback to both students and instructors about their progress in acquiring knowledge and skills. It allows students to identify areas of strength and weakness, enabling them to adjust their learning strategies and improve their performance. Instructors can monitor student progress and intervene when necessary, ensuring that learning objectives are being met.

Authentic Learning: PBL focuses on real-world problem-solving, and assessment aligns with this approach. Authentic assessments in PBL simulate real-life scenarios, requiring students to apply knowledge and skills to solve complex problems. This type of assessment helps students develop critical thinking, problem-solving, and decision-making abilities, which are highly valuable in professional contexts.

Engaging and Motivating: Assessment in PBL can be designed to engage and motivate students. By framing assessments as opportunities to demonstrate their abilities and showcase their learning, students become more actively involved in the learning process. This approach enhances student engagement and promotes intrinsic motivation.

Continuous Improvement: Regular assessment in PBL allows for ongoing reflection and adjustment of the instructional process. Through feedback and assessment data, instructors can identify areas where students are struggling and make necessary modifications to improve teaching and learning effectiveness. Additionally, assessment data can inform curriculum development and ensure the alignment of learning outcomes with the needs of the profession.

Evaluation often includes assessing the effectiveness of instructional strategies, the integration of PBL in the curriculum, and the overall attainment of program goals.

Program Improvement: Evaluation helps identify the strengths and weaknesses of the PBL program. It provides insights into the effectiveness of the instructional design, curriculum implementation, and the overall impact on student learning. Evaluation findings can inform program improvements, such as refining the PBL curriculum, enhancing faculty development, or adjusting assessment strategies.

Accountability and Quality Assurance: Evaluation ensures accountability and quality assurance in PBL. By systematically examining the program's outcomes and impact, educational institutions can demonstrate the effectiveness and value of the PBL approach to various stakeholders, such as accrediting bodies, employers, and students.

Evidence-Based Practice: Evaluation generates evidence about the impact and benefits of PBL. Research studies and evaluations contribute to the broader body of knowledge on PBL's effectiveness and can guide evidence-based decision-making in education. This knowledge helps inform educational policies, curriculum development, and instructional practices in PBL and beyond.

Assessment and evaluation play vital roles in problem-based learning. They provide feedback, monitor student progress, promote authentic learning, engage and motivate students, facilitate continuous improvement, and contribute to evidence-based practice. By incorporating effective assessment and evaluation strategies, educators can enhance the overall quality and effectiveness of the PBL experience for learners.

CHAPTER EIGHT
How to Implement PBL into the classroom

Problem-Based Learning (PBL) is a student-centered instructional approach that fosters critical thinking, problem-solving skills, and collaboration. By presenting students with real-world problems and encouraging active engagement, PBL promotes a deeper understanding of concepts and enhances the transfer of knowledge to practical applications. This guide provides a step-by-step approach to demonstrate Problem-Based Learning effectively in college classrooms.

Step 1: Define Learning Objectives Begin by clearly defining the learning objectives for the PBL activity. Identify the core concepts, skills, and knowledge that students should acquire through the problem-solving process. Align the objectives with the course curriculum to ensure relevance and coherence.

Step 2: Select a Real-World Problem Choose a real-world problem that is relevant to the course content and challenges students to think critically. The problem should be complex enough to require in-depth analysis but not overwhelmingly difficult. Consider incorporating interdisciplinary elements to encourage holistic thinking.

Step 3: Organize Student Groups Divide the students into small groups of 4-6 members. Aim for diversity in terms of skills, backgrounds, and perspectives within each group to encourage collaboration and different approaches to problem-solving.

Step 4: Introduce the Problem Present the problem to the students in an engaging and thought-provoking manner. Use real-life scenarios, case studies, or multimedia resources to provide context and stimulate interest. Allow students to ask clarifying questions to ensure a thorough understanding of the problem.

Step 5: Facilitate Self-Directed Learning Guide students in conducting research to gather information relevant to the problem. Encourage them to explore various sources, such as textbooks, academic journals, online databases, and expert interviews. Teach them effective research strategies and critical evaluation of information sources.

Step 6: Generate Hypotheses and Analyze the Problem Instruct students to generate hypotheses or possible solutions based on the information they have gathered. Encourage them to analyze the problem from different angles, consider alternative perspectives, and identify underlying assumptions or biases.

Step 7: Support Reflection and Discussion Facilitate regular reflection sessions where students can discuss their findings, insights, and challenges faced during the problem-solving process. Encourage them to articulate their thoughts, listen actively to others, and constructively critique ideas. These discussions promote metacognitive skills and deepen understanding.

Step 8: Provide Guidance and Feedback Act as a facilitator and guide throughout the PBL process. Offer assistance and resources when needed, but allow students to take ownership of their learning. Provide constructive feedback to individual groups to help them refine their thinking, problem-solving strategies, and communication skills.

Step 9: Develop a Final Product Encourage students to synthesize their learning into a final product that demonstrates their understanding and proposed solutions. This could take the form of a report, presentation, prototype, or multimedia project. Emphasize the importance of effective communication and clarity in conveying their ideas.

Step 10: Showcase and Reflect on Learning Allocate time for groups to present their final products to the class. Encourage peer evaluation and constructive feedback to foster a collaborative learning environment. Facilitate a reflective discussion where students can articulate their learning outcomes, challenges faced, and strategies employed. Encourage self-assessment and goal-setting for future learning.

Step 11: Assess Learning Outcomes Design appropriate assessment methods that align with the learning objectives and the nature of the PBL activity. Consider a combination of individual and group assessments, including written assignments, presentations, group dynamics evaluations, and self-reflection journals. Assess both the process (e.g., research, collaboration) and the product (e.g., final solution).

Step 12: Evaluate and Iterate Collect feedback from students about their experience with PBL and the effectiveness of the learning process. Reflect on the strengths and areas for improvement in the implementation of PBL. Use this feedback to refine future PBL activities and make adjustments to enhance the learning experience.

Problem-Based Learning provides an effective framework for engaging college students in active, student-centered learning. By following the steps outlined in this guide, instructors can successfully implement PBL in their college classrooms. By presenting students with authentic, real-world problems and fostering collaboration, critical thinking, and problem-solving skills, PBL enhances students' understanding and prepares them for future challenges in their academic and professional lives.

Unlike traditional teaching methods that rely heavily on lectures and memorization, PBL engages students in active learning, critical thinking, and problem-solving. This book aims to explore the significance of implementing PBL in the classroom and why it has become the preferred approach in prestigious universities.

1. *Active Learning and Student Engagement:* One of the key reasons why implementing PBL in the classroom is significant is its ability to promote active learning and enhance student engagement. Rather than passively receiving information, students become active participants in their own education. PBL involves posing real-world problems to students, encouraging them to explore and research the topic independently. By doing so, students take ownership of their learning, leading to increased motivation and a deeper understanding of the subject matter.

2. ***Development of Critical Thinking and Problem-Solving Skills:*** PBL fosters the development of critical thinking and problem-solving skills, which are crucial for success in higher education and beyond. When students tackle authentic problems, they are required to analyze information, think critically, and apply their knowledge to propose potential solutions. This approach allows them to develop skills such as information synthesis, decision-making, and effective communication, which are vital for addressing complex challenges in their future careers.

3. ***Application of Knowledge to Real-World Situations:*** Traditional teaching methods often fail to bridge the gap between theoretical knowledge and its practical application. PBL, on the other hand, emphasizes the application of knowledge to real-world situations. By engaging in problem-solving activities, students can see the relevance and applicability of what they are learning.

This connection to real-life scenarios not only enhances their understanding but also prepares them for the complexities they may encounter in their professional lives.

4. *Collaborative Learning and Interdisciplinary Approach:* PBL encourages collaborative learning and an interdisciplinary approach to education. In PBL classrooms, students work together in small groups, allowing them to engage in discussions, share ideas, and collaborate on finding solutions. This collaborative environment fosters teamwork, communication, and respect for diverse perspectives. Furthermore, PBL often integrates multiple disciplines, enabling students to develop a broader understanding of complex issues by drawing from various areas of knowledge.

5. *Long-Term Retention of Knowledge:* Studies have shown that PBL promotes long-term retention of knowledge compared to traditional teaching

methods. The active engagement and application of knowledge in real-world contexts facilitate deeper learning, making it more likely for students to remember and apply what they have learned even after the course has ended. This retention of knowledge is crucial for students' success in subsequent courses and their future professional endeavors.

6. ***Preparation for the Workforce:*** PBL aligns with the demands of the modern workforce, where employers increasingly seek individuals with critical thinking, problem-solving, and teamwork skills. By incorporating PBL in the classroom, prestigious universities ensure that their graduates are well-prepared to meet these expectations. Graduates who have experienced PBL are often better equipped to adapt to rapidly changing environments, tackle complex challenges, and contribute meaningfully to their organizations.

Implementing problem-based learning in the classroom is a significant approach that prestigious universities prefer due to its numerous benefits. By promoting active learning, critical thinking, and problem-solving skills, PBL engages students in their education, making the learning process more meaningful and impactful. The emphasis on real-world application, collaboration, and interdisciplinary learning prepares students for success in higher education and the workforce. As the educational landscape continues to evolve, the significance of PBL is likely to persist, fostering a generation of adaptable, skilled, and innovative individuals ready to tackle the challenges of the future.

Problem-based learning has gained significant recognition in higher education for its ability to engage students and prepare them for the challenges of the workforce. However, there is an ongoing debate regarding the ideal stage to introduce PBL, whether it should be implemented in K-12 education or reserved exclusively for higher education. This book aims to explore the benefits and considerations of introducing PBL at different educational levels and provide insights into the optimal starting point for its implementation.

Benefits of Introducing PBL in K-12 Education

Promoting Early Engagement: Introducing PBL in the early years of education helps foster a love for learning and active student engagement. By presenting real-world problems, students are encouraged to explore, question, and seek solutions. This approach cultivates curiosity, motivation, and a sense of ownership over their education.

Developing Essential Skills: PBL in K-12 education allows students to develop critical thinking, problem-solving, and collaboration skills at an early stage. These skills are foundational for academic success and essential for their personal and professional lives. By engaging in PBL from a young age, students can build a solid framework of skills that will benefit them throughout their educational journey.

Bridging Theory and Practice: Integrating PBL in K-12 education bridges the gap between theoretical knowledge and practical application. Students have the opportunity to apply what they learn to real-world scenarios, enhancing their understanding and developing a deeper appreciation for the subject matter. This experiential learning approach fosters a sense of relevance and prepares students for the challenges they may encounter in higher education and beyond.

Considerations for Implementing PBL in K-12 Education

Teacher Training and Support: Introducing PBL in K-12 education requires adequate teacher training and ongoing support. Teachers need to be proficient in designing and facilitating problem-based activities, guiding students through the process, and assessing their learning. Provision of professional development opportunities and resources is essential to ensure the successful implementation of PBL at this level.

Age-Appropriate Challenges:

Designing age-appropriate problems and ensuring the right level of complexity can be a challenge in K-12 education. Careful consideration must be given to align the problems with students' cognitive abilities, allowing them to grasp the concepts and engage effectively. Adjusting the difficulty level and scaffolding the learning process are crucial to ensure optimal learning outcomes.

Benefits of Introducing PBL in Higher Education

Enhancing Critical Thinking and Problem-Solving Skills: Higher education is an ideal setting for implementing PBL due to its emphasis on critical thinking and problem-solving. By engaging students in authentic, complex problems, PBL enhances their ability to analyze information, think critically, and propose innovative solutions. These skills are vital for success in higher education and the professional world.

Preparing for Professional Challenges: PBL in higher education aligns with the demands of the modern workforce. It prepares students for real-world challenges by providing opportunities to collaborate, communicate, and think creatively. By working on complex, interdisciplinary problems, students develop the adaptability and resilience needed to thrive in their future careers.

Fostering Lifelong Learning: Introducing PBL in higher education cultivates a mindset of lifelong learning. Students become self-directed learners, equipped with the skills to seek out knowledge, analyze information, and continue their education beyond the confines of the classroom. PBL nurtures a sense of curiosity, critical inquiry, and a passion for continued growth and development.

Considerations for Implementing PBL in Higher Education

Curriculum Integration: Implementing PBL in higher education requires careful integration with the curriculum. A well-designed PBL approach should complement existing courses, ensuring that the learning outcomes and objectives are met. Collaboration among faculty members, instructional designers, and curriculum developers is crucial to achieve a seamless integration of PBL.

Assessment Strategies: Developing appropriate assessment strategies for PBL in higher education is essential to measure students' understanding and progress. The assessment should align with the objectives of PBL, focusing on the application of knowledge, critical thinking, and problem-solving skills. A mix of formative and summative assessments, including group presentations, portfolios, and reflections, can effectively evaluate students' learning outcomes.

Both K-12 education and higher education can benefit from the introduction of problem-based learning. Implementing PBL in K-12 education promotes early engagement, skill development, and the bridging of theory and practice. It lays a solid foundation for students to become active learners, critical thinkers, and collaborative problem solvers. On the other hand, PBL in higher education enhances critical thinking, problem-solving skills, and prepares students for the complexities of the workforce. It fosters a lifelong learning mindset and equips students with the skills necessary for success in their careers. Ultimately, the decision to introduce PBL at a particular educational level depends on the specific context, resources, and goals of the educational institution. However, by considering the benefits and considerations outlined above, educators and policymakers can make informed decisions regarding the optimal starting point for implementing problem-based learning.

CHAPTER NINE
Problem-Based Learning in Disciplines

Problem-Based Learning (PBL) is an educational approach that emphasizes active learning and problem-solving. It involves presenting students with authentic, real-world problems or scenarios and guiding them through the process of finding solutions. PBL has gained popularity across various disciplines, including teaching, accounting, finance, data analytics, business management, economics, engineering, higher education administration, computer science, psychology, and communications. In this comprehensive book, we will explore how PBL is implemented and its benefits in each of these fields.

Problem-Based Learning in Teaching

PBL offers a student-centered approach to teaching, enabling educators to foster critical thinking, problem-solving, and collaboration skills. In a PBL classroom, teachers act as facilitators, guiding students through the process of identifying, analyzing, and solving problems. By integrating real-world issues into the curriculum, PBL helps students connect theoretical knowledge to practical applications. It promotes a deeper understanding of concepts and enhances students' ability to transfer knowledge to different contexts.

Problem-Based Learning in Accounting and Finance

Accounting and finance require analytical thinking and the ability to apply theoretical concepts to practical scenarios. PBL is an ideal approach to develop these skills. Students can engage in hands-on activities, such as analyzing financial statements, solving complex accounting problems, or evaluating investment opportunities. PBL promotes critical thinking, attention to detail, and a deeper understanding of financial principles. It also encourages teamwork and communication, essential for future professionals in these fields.

Problem-Based Learning in Data Analytics

Data analytics is a rapidly evolving field that demands proficiency in problem-solving and data interpretation. PBL helps students develop these skills by presenting them with real-world data sets and challenging problems to solve. Through PBL, students learn to manipulate and analyze data, apply statistical methods, and draw meaningful insights. PBL also encourages students to explore different data analysis techniques and tools, promoting adaptability and creativity in solving complex problems.

Problem-Based Learning in Business Management

Business management involves decision-making, problem-solving, and effective leadership. PBL allows students to engage in real-life business scenarios, such as developing marketing strategies, analyzing market trends, or solving organizational challenges. By working collaboratively in teams, students develop critical thinking, communication, and negotiation skills. PBL also enhances their ability to analyze business problems from multiple perspectives, preparing them for managerial roles in diverse industries.

Problem-Based Learning in Economics

Economics encompasses the study of production, distribution, and consumption of goods and services. PBL in economics offers students an opportunity to explore economic concepts through practical applications. By examining real-world economic issues, such as unemployment, inflation, or international trade, students gain a deeper understanding of economic theories and their implications. PBL enhances their analytical skills, ability to collect and interpret data, and critical thinking capabilities.

Problem-Based Learning in Engineering

Engineering education requires students to solve complex problems, design innovative solutions, and collaborate effectively. PBL provides a platform for students to apply engineering principles to real-world challenges. Whether it's designing a sustainable energy system or constructing a bridge, PBL engages students in hands-on problem-solving experiences. It promotes creativity, critical thinking, teamwork, and communication skills, preparing future engineers to tackle complex engineering problems.

Problem-Based Learning in Higher Education Administration

In higher education administration, PBL can enhance the learning experience of both administrators and students. PBL encourages administrators to analyze and solve complex issues related to curriculum development, student engagement, or resource allocation. By applying PBL principles, administrators can foster innovation, collaboration, and continuous improvement within their institutions. For students pursuing higher education administration, PBL helps develop strategic thinking, problem-solving, and decision-making skills.

Problem-Based Learning in Computer Science

Computer science is a field that requires problem-solving, algorithmic thinking, and programming skills. PBL enables students to develop these competencies by engaging in hands-on coding projects and solving real-world programming challenges. By working collaboratively, students learn to analyze problems, break them down into smaller tasks, and develop efficient solutions. PBL in computer science fosters creativity, critical thinking, and adaptability, preparing students for diverse careers in technology.

Problem-Based Learning in Psychology

Psychology education involves understanding human behavior, conducting research, and applying theories to practical situations. PBL offers students an opportunity to explore psychological concepts through real-world case studies or experiments. By engaging in problem-solving activities, students develop critical thinking, research, and analytical skills. PBL also enhances their ability to apply psychological theories to diverse contexts, such as clinical settings, organizational environments, or educational settings.

Problem-Based Learning in Communications

Communications is a field that relies on effective problem-solving, critical thinking, and interpersonal skills. PBL in communications allows students to tackle real-world communication challenges, such as developing persuasive campaigns, analyzing media trends, or resolving conflicts. By working in teams, students develop collaboration, leadership, and presentation skills. PBL also enhances their ability to critically evaluate and apply communication theories and strategies.

Problem-Based Learning (PBL) is a versatile approach that can be effectively applied across various disciplines in education. Whether it's teaching, accounting, finance, data analytics, business management, economics, engineering, higher education administration, computer science, psychology, or communications, PBL offers a student-centered and practical approach to learning. By engaging in problem-solving activities, students develop critical thinking, collaboration, and communication skills, preparing them for real-world challenges in their chosen fields. As educators and institutions continue to embrace PBL, it becomes an increasingly valuable tool for enhancing education and skill development in diverse domains.

Problem Based Learning – By College Major

Problem-based learning (PBL) is a student-centered instructional approach that has gained popularity across various disciplines in higher education. PBL involves presenting students with real-world problems or scenarios and challenging them to find solutions through collaborative and active learning. This teaching methodology is particularly effective for majors such as accounting, finance, business management, business, economics, engineering, higher education, computer science, and psychology. Let's explore how PBL can benefit each of these majors:

1. *Accounting Major:* PBL can enhance an accounting student's critical thinking and problem-solving skills by exposing them to complex financial scenarios. By working on realistic cases, students can apply their theoretical knowledge to practical situations, analyze financial statements, and make informed

decisions. PBL encourages students to collaborate, communicate effectively, and develop a deep understanding of accounting principles and ethical considerations.
2. *Finance Major:* PBL provides finance students with opportunities to explore financial markets, investment strategies, and risk management through hands-on experiences. By analyzing real financial data and considering various economic factors, students can develop their analytical and decision-making skills. PBL also encourages students to think critically about financial issues, such as capital budgeting, mergers and acquisitions, and portfolio management.
3. *Business Management Major:* PBL is highly suitable for business management students as it prepares them to tackle complex challenges faced by organizations. Through PBL, students can develop skills in strategic thinking, problem-solving, and decision-making. They can work on cases related to organizational behavior, leadership, marketing, and operations management,

which helps them understand the multifaceted nature of managing a business.
4. ***Business and Economics Major:*** PBL is an effective approach for business and economics students to develop a comprehensive understanding of economic principles and their practical applications. By engaging in PBL activities, students can explore concepts like supply and demand, market competition, pricing strategies, and macroeconomic policies. They can analyze real-world economic scenarios, assess the implications of various economic factors, and propose viable solutions.
5. ***Engineering Major:*** PBL is particularly beneficial for engineering majors as it promotes problem-solving skills and enhances their ability to apply engineering principles in practical situations. By working on real engineering challenges, students can learn to design solutions, conduct experiments, and evaluate the feasibility and sustainability of their designs. PBL

also fosters teamwork, communication, and project management skills, which are essential in engineering practice.
6. *Higher Education Major:* PBL can be instrumental in preparing future educators and administrators in higher education. By engaging in PBL activities, higher education majors can explore the complexities of teaching and learning, curriculum development, and educational leadership. They can analyze educational issues, design innovative instructional strategies, and evaluate their effectiveness. PBL encourages reflection, collaboration, and the development of pedagogical skills.
7. *Computer Science Major:* PBL is highly effective in computer science education as it mirrors the problem-solving nature of the field. Students can engage in programming challenges, software development projects, and data analysis tasks. PBL helps computer science majors develop their coding skills, logical reasoning, and algorithmic thinking. It also promotes teamwork and

communication, which are crucial for successful software development.

8. *Psychology Major:* PBL can be used to enhance the learning experience of psychology students by immersing them in real-world scenarios and ethical dilemmas. Students can analyze case studies, conduct research, and develop interventions or treatment plans. PBL helps psychology majors apply psychological theories, research methods, and ethical principles to understand human behavior and address psychological issues. It also fosters critical thinking, empathy, and effective communication skills.

Problem-based learning offers numerous benefits to students pursuing various majors. It enhances critical thinking, problem-solving, and collaboration skills while bridging the gap between theoretical knowledge and practical applications. PBL is a valuable teaching methodology that can effectively prepare students for their future careers in accounting, finance, business management, business, economics, engineering, higher education, computer science, and psychology.

Underutilization of Problem-Based Learning in the Classroom

Despite its numerous benefits, PBL is not yet widely embraced by professors in various academic institutions. This book aims to examine the reasons behind the underutilization of PBL by professors, highlighting 30 common barriers that hinder its implementation. By understanding these challenges, we can work towards overcoming them and fostering a greater adoption of PBL in higher education.

1. **Lack of Familiarity:** Professors may be unfamiliar with the concept of PBL or may not have received adequate training on its implementation. This lack of familiarity can deter them from adopting PBL as a teaching method.

2. **Time Constraints:** PBL requires significant time investment, both in designing and facilitating the learning process. Professors often face time

constraints due to heavy workloads and limited resources, making it challenging to incorporate PBL effectively.

3. **Resistance to Change:** Some professors may be resistant to change, preferring traditional lecture-based methods that they are comfortable with. Implementing PBL requires a shift in mindset and teaching strategies, which can be met with resistance.

4. **Assessment Challenges:** Assessing student learning in PBL can be complex, as it involves evaluating not only knowledge acquisition but also problem-solving skills and teamwork. Professors may struggle with developing appropriate assessment methods for PBL.

5. **Lack of Institutional Support:** The lack of institutional support, both in terms of resources and recognition, can hinder professors from implementing PBL. Without adequate support, professors

may be reluctant to invest time and effort in adopting a new teaching approach.

6. **Large Class Sizes:** PBL is more effective in smaller class sizes that facilitate meaningful interactions. Professors may find it challenging to implement PBL in large classes, where individualized attention and group dynamics become more difficult to manage.

7. **Limited Collaboration Opportunities:** PBL relies heavily on collaboration among students. However, limited opportunities for collaboration within the curriculum or rigid departmental structures may discourage professors from adopting PBL.

8. **Lack of Student Preparedness:** Implementing PBL requires students to possess certain foundational knowledge and skills. Professors may hesitate to adopt PBL if they believe that students are not adequately prepared to engage in problem-solving activities.

9. **Resource Constraints:** PBL often requires additional resources such as technology, materials, and physical space for group work. Limited access to these resources can pose a barrier to implementing PBL in some academic settings.

10. **Perception of Inefficiency:** Some professors may perceive PBL as an inefficient teaching method, as it requires more time for active learning and group discussions. This perception can discourage them from adopting PBL, particularly in content-heavy courses.

11. **Faculty Resistance:** The resistance to PBL may not only come from individual professors but also from faculty members who are not supportive of this pedagogical approach. A lack of consensus among faculty can impede the implementation of PBL across a department or institution.

12. **Lack of Training Opportunities:** Professors may have a genuine interest in implementing PBL but lack the necessary training and professional development opportunities. Without proper training, they may feel ill-equipped to design and facilitate PBL experiences effectively.

13. **Student Resistance:** Students who are accustomed to traditional lecture-based instruction may resist the transition to PBL. Professors may be hesitant to implement PBL if they anticipate student resistance or negative evaluations.

14. **Content Coverage Concerns**: Professors may worry that implementing PBL could lead to insufficient coverage of course content. Balancing content coverage with the active learning experiences inherent in PBL can be a challenge.

15. **Disciplinary Constraints:** Certain disciplines or subjects may be perceived as less conducive to PBL due to their content or methodology. Professors in these disciplines may feel limited in their ability to implement PBL effectively.

16. **Perceived Workload:** Professors may perceive PBL as requiring additional effort and preparation compared to traditional lecture-based instruction. This perception of an increased workload can discourage them from embracing PBL.

17. **Lack of Supportive Infrastructure:** Implementing PBL successfully requires a supportive infrastructure that includes technological support, physical spaces for collaborative work, and administrative policies that facilitate active learning. Without such infrastructure, professors may find it challenging to adopt PBL.

18. **Limited Evaluation and Promotion Criteria:** The evaluation and promotion criteria in academic institutions often prioritize research output rather than teaching innovation. This lack of recognition for PBL can discourage professors from investing time and effort in adopting this pedagogical approach.

19. **Student Diversity and Varied Learning Needs:** PBL relies on active student participation, but student diversity and varied learning needs can pose challenges. Professors may hesitate to adopt PBL if they feel it does not cater to the diverse needs of their students.

20. **Resistance from Peers:** Professors who are enthusiastic about implementing PBL may face resistance or skepticism from their peers who are not yet convinced of its efficacy. This resistance from colleagues can hinder the widespread adoption of PBL.

21. **Limited Research on Discipline-Specific PBL:** Some academic disciplines may have limited research or evidence on the effectiveness of PBL within their specific field. Professors may be hesitant to implement PBL without sufficient discipline-specific evidence.

22. **Faculty Workload Allocation:** In institutions where faculty workload allocation is primarily based on teaching hours, professors may hesitate to adopt PBL, as it may require more time and effort compared to traditional instruction.

23. **Lack of Collaboration with Employers and Industry:** PBL is strengthened by collaboration with employers and industry partners. However, limited connections and collaborations between academia and the professional world can hinder the implementation of PBL.

24. **Limited Availability of PBL Resources:** Professors may find it challenging to locate and access high-quality PBL resources and materials that are tailored to their specific courses or disciplines.

25. **Limited Incentives for PBL Implementation:** The lack of incentives, rewards, or recognition for professors who adopt PBL can be a significant barrier. Without appropriate incentives, professors may be less motivated to invest in PBL.

26. **Perceived Lack of Rigor:** Some professors may perceive PBL as lacking the rigor of traditional instruction, particularly in terms of content delivery and assessment. This perception can lead them to overlook the benefits of PBL.

27. **Limited Support for Continuous Improvement:** Implementing PBL requires ongoing reflection and continuous improvement. Professors may be discouraged from adopting PBL

if they feel they lack the necessary support and feedback mechanisms to refine their practice.

28. **Limited Interdisciplinary Collaboration:** PBL often involves interdisciplinary collaboration, which can be challenging in institutions with disciplinary silos. Lack of opportunities for interdisciplinary collaboration can impede the implementation of PBL.

29. **Resistance from Accrediting Bodies:** Accrediting bodies that evaluate academic programs may not yet fully embrace PBL or may have specific criteria that are challenging to meet within a PBL framework. This resistance can discourage professors from adopting PBL.

30. **Lack of Evidence-Based Support:** Despite the growing body of research supporting the effectiveness of PBL, some professors may remain skeptical due to a lack of discipline-specific

evidence or familiarity with the research literature.

The underutilization of Problem-Based Learning (PBL) by professors in higher education can be attributed to various barriers, ranging from resistance to change and limited resources to assessment challenges and disciplinary constraints. Addressing these barriers requires a comprehensive approach that includes faculty training, institutional support, infrastructure development, and incentives for innovation in teaching. By recognizing and overcoming these challenges, we can foster a broader adoption of PBL, leading to more student-centered, engaging, and effective educational experiences.

Improving the Utilization of Problem-Based Learning by Professors

Problem-Based Learning (PBL) holds immense potential in transforming education, fostering critical thinking, collaboration, and problem-solving skills among students. To address the barriers that hinder its utilization by professors, several strategies can be employed. This book outlines key approaches to improving the adoption of PBL in higher education.

1. **Professional Development and Training:** Offering comprehensive professional development programs and training sessions can equip professors with the necessary knowledge and skills to effectively implement PBL. Workshops, seminars, and online resources can provide guidance on designing PBL experiences, assessing student learning, and managing group dynamics.

2. **Supportive Institutional Policies**: Institutions can promote the adoption of PBL by incorporating supportive policies and practices. This includes recognizing and rewarding professors who embrace innovative teaching methods, revising promotion criteria to value teaching excellence, and allocating resources for faculty development and infrastructure necessary for PBL implementation.

3. **Collaborative Communities of Practice:** Facilitating communities of practice where professors can share experiences, exchange ideas, and collaborate on PBL initiatives can foster a supportive environment. Regular meetings, discussion forums, and interdisciplinary collaborations encourage peer-to-peer learning and provide a platform for overcoming challenges associated with PBL implementation.

4. **Departmental and Institutional Leadership**: Effective leadership at the departmental and institutional levels is crucial for promoting PBL. Leaders can advocate for the benefits of PBL, encourage its implementation, and allocate resources to support faculty members in their endeavors. Establishing PBL champions within departments can also drive enthusiasm and provide mentorship to faculty members.

5. **Flexible Curriculum Design:** Institutions can incorporate flexibility into their curriculum design to accommodate PBL experiences. By allowing for dedicated PBL modules or courses, faculty members can integrate problem-solving activities seamlessly into the curriculum without compromising content coverage. Flexibility also facilitates interdisciplinary collaboration and encourages faculty members to explore PBL approaches tailored to their disciplines.

6. **Student Engagement and Support**: Engaging students as partners in the learning process is crucial for the success of PBL. Providing students with orientation sessions on PBL, explaining its benefits, and involving them in the co-creation of learning experiences can enhance their motivation and readiness to engage in PBL activities. Institutions can also offer resources such as learning centers, peer tutoring, and online platforms to support students'

development of problem-solving and collaborative skills.

7. **Faculty-Student Feedback Mechanisms:** Establishing regular feedback mechanisms between faculty members and students can provide valuable insights into the effectiveness of PBL implementations. Feedback surveys, focus groups, and individual discussions can help identify areas for improvement, gauge student perceptions of PBL, and inform ongoing faculty development efforts.

8. **Integration of Technology:** Leveraging technology can enhance the implementation of PBL. Virtual collaboration tools, online platforms for resource sharing, and multimedia resources can facilitate communication and information exchange among students and professors. Additionally, utilizing learning management systems can streamline the organization and management of PBL activities.

9. **Collaboration with Employers and Industry**: Collaborating with employers and industry professionals can enhance the authenticity and relevance of PBL experiences. Engaging external stakeholders in designing PBL scenarios, providing real-world challenges, and participating in assessments can bridge the gap between academia and the professional world, reinforcing the value of PBL.

10. **Evidence-Based Research and Dissemination**: Conducting and disseminating discipline-specific research on the effectiveness of PBL can address the lack of evidence in some fields. Encouraging faculty members to engage in research on PBL, sharing successful case studies, and disseminating findings through conferences, journals, and online platforms can contribute to the knowledge base and encourage wider adoption.

11. **Long-Term Evaluation and Continuous** Improvement: Establishing mechanisms for long-term evaluation and continuous improvement of PBL implementations can ensure its effectiveness. Monitoring student outcomes, soliciting feedback from faculty members, and conducting systematic evaluations can provide insights into the strengths and weaknesses of PBL initiatives, leading to iterative improvements over time.

12. **Collaboration Across Disciplines:** Encouraging collaboration and interdisciplinary dialogue among faculty members from different disciplines can broaden perspectives on PBL. Sharing best practices, lessons learned, and interdisciplinary research findings can inspire innovation and foster a supportive culture that transcends disciplinary boundaries.

Improving the utilization of Problem-Based Learning (PBL) by professors requires a multifaceted approach that encompasses professional development, supportive institutional policies, collaborative communities of practice, and student engagement. By fostering a culture that values innovative teaching methods, providing resources and support, and promoting ongoing evaluation and improvement, we can overcome barriers and facilitate the widespread adoption of PBL in higher education, ultimately enhancing the quality of learning experiences for students.

CHAPTER TEN
Foundation Theorists of Problem Based Learning

Problem-based learning (PBL) is an instructional approach that emphasizes active learning and critical thinking skills by presenting students with authentic, complex problems to solve. While PBL has evolved and been implemented in various educational settings, it owes its foundation to the work of several influential theorists. This book will examine the lives and theories of three prominent figures in the development of problem-based learning: Howard Barrows, Hilda Taba, and Jerome Bruner, just to name a few.

Howard Barrows: Howard Barrows (1922-2016) was an American physician and medical educator who is widely recognized as one of the pioneers of PBL. He dedicated his career to improving medical education and finding innovative ways to train competent and compassionate physicians. Howard Barrows:

Barrows is often regarded as the "father of PBL." His work in the 1960s and 1970s laid the foundation for PBL methodology. Barrows emphasized the importance of authentic problems and the role of facilitators in guiding students through the problem-solving process.

Barrows's interest in PBL emerged from his dissatisfaction with traditional medical education, which relied heavily on lectures and rote memorization. He believed that medical students needed to actively engage with real-world problems to develop clinical reasoning skills and a deeper understanding of medical concepts.

Barrows's theory of problem-based learning focused on the concept of "ill-structured problems." According to him, these problems should reflect the complexity and ambiguity of real-world situations, challenging students to analyze, evaluate, and apply knowledge to develop solutions. He believed that PBL could foster self-directed learning and collaboration among students, as they worked together to explore different perspectives and propose solutions.

Barrows also emphasized the role of the tutor or facilitator in PBL. He believed that tutors should guide students through the learning process, asking probing questions, providing feedback, and helping students reflect on their learning experiences. Barrows' work laid the foundation for the implementation of PBL in medical education, and his ideas have influenced the application of PBL in other disciplines as well.

Hilda Taba: Hilda Taba (1902-1967) was an Estonian-born American educator and curriculum theorist. Although not directly associated with the medical field like Barrows, Taba made significant contributions to the development of problem-based learning in general education settings.

Taba's theory of curriculum development focused on the idea of "inductive reasoning," which aligns closely with the principles of problem-based learning. She advocated for an instructional approach that began with students' firsthand experiences and observations, allowing them to identify problems and generate hypotheses. Taba believed that this approach would promote active engagement, critical thinking, and the construction of meaningful knowledge.

In Taba's view, curriculum development should follow a logical sequence of steps: (1) formulation of objectives, (2) organization of content, (3) selection of learning experiences, and (4) evaluation of student learning. Through this process, teachers would guide students in exploring relevant problems and discovering knowledge through their own inquiries.

Taba's work highlighted the importance of integrating problem-solving and critical thinking skills into the curriculum. She believed that education should empower students to become active, lifelong learners who can apply their knowledge to real-world situations. Taba's ideas have greatly influenced the implementation of PBL in general education, where students are exposed to authentic problems and encouraged to develop their problem-solving skills.

Jerome Bruner: Jerome Bruner (1915-2016) was an influential American psychologist and cognitive theorist who made significant contributions to the field of education. His work on cognitive psychology and learning theory has had a profound impact on various educational approaches, including problem-based learning.

Bruner's theory of constructivism emphasized the active role of learners in constructing knowledge through their interactions with the environment. He argued that learners should be actively involved in the process of meaning-making, rather than being passive recipients of information. This idea aligns well with the principles of problem-based learning, where students actively engage with authentic problems and construct their understanding of the subject matter.

Bruner also introduced the concept of the "spiral curriculum," which suggests that learning should be structured in a way that allows for revisiting and deepening understanding over time. He believed that complex topics should be presented in a scaffolded manner, gradually increasing in complexity and depth. This approach encourages students to build upon their prior knowledge and make connections between different concepts and ideas.

Bruner's work highlighted the importance of narrative and storytelling in education. He argued that narratives provide a powerful framework for organizing and making sense of information. In the context of problem-based learning, narratives can be used to contextualize problems, making them more engaging and meaningful for students.

Overall, the theories of Howard Barrows, Hilda Taba, and Jerome Bruner have significantly influenced the development and implementation of problem-based learning. Barrows's emphasis on ill-structured problems and the role of tutors, Taba's focus on inductive reasoning and problem-solving skills in curriculum development, and Bruner's constructivist perspective and the spiral curriculum concept have all shaped the principles and practices of PBL in different educational contexts.

Their collective contributions have paved the way for a learner-centered, inquiry-based approach to education that promotes critical thinking, collaboration, and the application of knowledge to real-world problems. It emphasizes active, student-centered learning through the exploration and resolution of real-world problems. This book aims to provide an extensive review of twenty foundation theorists whose work has significantly influenced the development and implementation of PBL. By understanding the theories and contributions of these scholars, we can gain insights into the underlying principles of PBL and its impact on education.

John Dewey: Although not directly associated with PBL, Dewey's progressive educational philosophy influenced the development of student-centered approaches. His emphasis on experiential learning and problem-solving aligns closely with the principles of PBL.

Jean Piaget: Piaget's constructivist theory of cognitive development provides the theoretical basis for PBL. His work emphasizes that learning is an active process, and learners construct knowledge through their interactions with the environment.

Lev Vygotsky: Vygotsky's sociocultural theory emphasizes the role of social interaction in learning. His concept of the Zone of Proximal Development aligns with the collaborative nature of PBL, as students work together to solve problems and support each other's learning.

Jerome Bruner: Bruner's work on constructivism and discovery learning has influenced PBL. His theory emphasizes the importance of active engagement, inquiry, and problem-solving in learning.

Albert Bandura: Bandura's social learning theory emphasizes the role of observational learning and modeling. In PBL, students observe and learn from their peers, as well as from expert facilitators, through collaborative problem-solving activities.

Carl Rogers: Rogers' person-centered approach to learning and education is closely aligned with the student-centered nature of PBL. His emphasis on individual autonomy, self-directed learning, and supportive environments resonates with the PBL philosophy.

Donald Schön: Schön's work on reflective practice is relevant to PBL. His concept of "reflection-in-action" highlights the importance of continuous reflection and adjustment during problem-solving, enabling learners to develop their problem-solving skills.

David Kolb: Kolb's experiential learning theory emphasizes the cyclical nature of learning, where learners engage in concrete experiences, reflect on them, conceptualize their observations, and apply their new knowledge. PBL aligns with Kolb's cycle by engaging students in active problem-solving experiences.

Roger Saljo: Saljo's work on learning in communities focuses on the social and collaborative aspects of learning. PBL, with its emphasis on teamwork and collaboration, aligns with Saljo's ideas of learning as a social and interactive process.

Ann Brown and Joseph Campione: Brown and Campione's theory of situated cognition emphasizes the importance of learning in authentic contexts. PBL's use of real-world problems enables students to apply their knowledge and skills in meaningful and relevant ways.

John Savery and Thomas Duffy: Savery and Duffy proposed a framework for problem-based learning that emphasizes authentic problems, collaborative learning, and learner autonomy. Their work provides a comprehensive framework for designing and implementing PBL experiences.

Lillian Bridwell-Bowles: Bridwell-Bowles' work on instructional design and problem-solving models has influenced the design of PBL curricula. Her focus on defining problem-solving processes and strategies aligns with the structure and methodology of PBL.

Maggi Savin-Baden: Savin-Baden's research focuses on the role of emotions in learning, including the emotional aspects of problem-solving. Her work highlights the importance of addressing learners' emotional responses during PBL activities.

Gilly Salmon: Salmon's work on e-learning and online communities has influenced the integration of technology in PBL. Her research on the use of online platforms and virtual environments in facilitating collaborative learning is relevant to PBL implementations.

Thomas Angelo and K. Patricia Cross: Angelo and Cross's work on classroom assessment techniques provides valuable insights for assessing learning outcomes in PBL. Their emphasis on formative assessment aligns with the iterative nature of PBL.

Helen Beetham: Beetham's research focuses on digital pedagogies and the integration of technology in education. Her work provides guidance on the effective use of digital tools and resources in PBL contexts.

Diana Laurillard: Laurillard's work on the conversational framework for learning emphasizes the importance of dialogue and interaction in the learning process. Her ideas can be applied to the facilitation of group discussions and reflections in PBL.

David Boud: Boud's research on reflective practice and self-regulated learning aligns with the goals of PBL. His emphasis on critical reflection and metacognitive skills development is relevant to the problem-solving process in PBL.

Randy Garrison: Garrison's work on online learning communities and communities of inquiry provides insights into the design and facilitation of collaborative learning experiences in PBL, particularly in online and blended learning environments.

The work of these foundation theorists has significantly contributed to the development and implementation of Problem-Based Learning (PBL). Their theories and research on constructivism, collaborative learning, reflective practice, authentic contexts, and assessment have shaped the principles and methodologies of PBL. By understanding their contributions, educators can effectively design and facilitate PBL experiences, fostering active, student-centered learning and preparing students for the complexities of real-world problem-solving.

The Value and Appreciation of Problem-Based Learning Theorists' Work

Problem-Based Learning (PBL) theorists have made significant contributions to education by developing a framework that promotes active learning, critical thinking, and problem-solving skills. Their work provides a solid foundation for educators and learners to engage in meaningful and authentic learning experiences. This book explores the reasons why the work of PBL theorists should be used and appreciated, highlighting the impact they have on teaching and learning practices.

1. ***Promoting Student-Centered Education:*** PBL theorists have shifted the focus of education from passive learning to active engagement. Their

work emphasizes the importance of student-centered approaches, where learners take ownership of their learning process. By appreciating their work, educators can create student-centered environments that foster curiosity, exploration, and a sense of agency among learners.

2. *Developing Critical Thinking Skills:* PBL theorists recognize the value of critical thinking in problem-solving. Their work emphasizes the development of analytical and evaluative skills necessary for real-world challenges. By utilizing their theories, educators can design learning experiences that encourage students to think critically, analyze information, and make informed decisions.

3. *Enhancing Problem-Solving Abilities:* **PBL** theorists have developed frameworks that enable learners to tackle complex problems. By appreciating their work, educators can implement PBL methodologies that facilitate the

acquisition of problem-solving skills. Students learn to identify problems, conduct research, propose solutions, and evaluate their effectiveness. These skills are crucial in preparing students for the challenges they will encounter in their personal and professional lives.

4. *Fostering Collaboration and Communication:* PBL theorists emphasize the importance of collaboration and communication in the learning process. By implementing their theories, educators can create opportunities for students to work collaboratively, exchange ideas, and engage in meaningful discussions. This collaborative environment nurtures effective communication skills, teamwork, and the ability to work productively in diverse groups.

5. *Encouraging Lifelong Learning:* The work of PBL theorists promotes a lifelong learning mindset. By appreciating their contributions, educators can inspire learners to become

self-directed and motivated in seeking knowledge beyond the classroom. PBL methodologies encourage learners to be curious, engage in ongoing reflection, and continuously expand their understanding of various subjects.

6. ***Bridging Theory and Practice:*** PBL theorists recognize the importance of applying theoretical knowledge to real-world contexts. By incorporating their work, educators can design learning experiences that bridge the gap between theory and practice. Learners engage in authentic problem-solving scenarios, enabling them to transfer knowledge, skills, and strategies to real-life situations.

7. ***Emphasizing Relevance and Engagement:*** PBL theorists understand the significance of relevance and engagement in effective learning. By appreciating their work, educators can design learning experiences that connect with learners' interests, experiences, and aspirations. PBL methodologies provide

a meaningful context that motivates students to actively engage in the learning process.

8. ***Embracing Innovation and Technology:*** PBL theorists recognize the potential of technology in enhancing learning experiences. By utilizing their work, educators can integrate innovative technologies into PBL methodologies, enabling learners to access vast resources, collaborate globally, and engage with digital tools that support problem-solving and critical thinking.

9. ***Nurturing Self-Reflection and Metacognition:*** PBL theorists emphasize the importance of self-reflection and metacognitive skills. By appreciating their work, educators can incorporate reflective practices into PBL activities, encouraging students to evaluate their learning process, identify strengths and weaknesses, and develop self-awareness. Metacognitive skills empower learners to become

independent and self-regulated in their learning journey.

10. **Preparing Students for the Future:** The work of PBL theorists aligns with the demands of the 21st-century workforce. By utilizing their theories, educators can equip students with the essential skills needed for future success, such as critical thinking, problem-solving, collaboration, communication, and adaptability. Appreciating their work ensures that education remains relevant and responsive to the evolving needs of society.

The work of Problem-Based Learning theorists has revolutionized education by promoting student-centered learning, critical thinking, and problem-solving skills. Their contributions have paved the way for innovative teaching methodologies that engage learners, foster collaboration, and nurture lifelong learning. By appreciating their work, educators can create transformative learning environments that prepare students for the challenges and opportunities of the future.

CHAPTER ELEVEN
Problem Based Learning in the Work Environment

Problem-based learning (PBL) is a student-centered instructional approach that encourages learners to solve real-world problems collaboratively. While PBL is commonly associated with educational settings, you can also apply its principles and methods to enhance learning and problem-solving in a work environment. Here are some steps to apply problem-based learning on the job:

1. ***Identify a relevant problem:*** Start by identifying a problem or challenge that you or your team need to address in your work. The problem should be authentic, meaningful, and align with your work objectives. It could be a process improvement, a customer issue, a new project, or any other work-related problem.

2. ***Formulate problem statements*:** Clearly articulate the problem in the form of problem statements. These statements should describe the problem succinctly, focusing on the key aspects that need to be addressed. Ensure that the problem statements are specific, actionable, and measurable.

3. ***Organize a problem-solving team:*** Assemble a diverse team of individuals who have relevant expertise and can contribute to solving the problem. Ideally, the team should include individuals with different perspectives and skills to foster creative thinking and collaboration.

4. ***Define learning objectives:*** Determine what you and your team aim to learn through the problem-solving process. These learning objectives could be both knowledge-based (e.g., understanding a specific concept or process) and skill-based (e.g., improving critical thinking or decision-making skills).

5. *Research and analyze:* Encourage the team to research and gather relevant information related to the problem. This may involve conducting interviews, collecting data, reviewing literature, or consulting experts. Analyze the information collected to gain insights into the problem's causes, implications, and potential solutions.

6. *Generate hypotheses and solutions:* Based on the analysis, have the team generate hypotheses or potential solutions to the problem. Encourage brainstorming and creative thinking to explore various possibilities. Evaluate the feasibility, potential outcomes, and risks associated with each hypothesis or solution.

7. *Plan and implement actions:* Develop an action plan that outlines the steps and resources required to test or implement the selected solutions. Divide tasks among team members, set deadlines, and establish a process for monitoring progress. Emphasize collaboration,

feedback, and iteration during the implementation phase.

8. ***Reflect and evaluate:*** After implementing the solutions, engage in reflection and evaluation to assess the effectiveness of the chosen approach. Discuss what worked well, what could be improved, and what lessons were learned. Use this feedback to refine strategies and enhance future problem-solving endeavors.

9. ***Share knowledge and disseminate results:*** Document the problem-solving process, findings, and outcomes to capture the knowledge and insights gained. Share this information within your team, department, or organization to promote organizational learning and foster continuous improvement.

By following these steps, you can apply problem-based learning principles in your job, promoting critical thinking, collaboration, and innovative problem-solving. Remember to adapt the process to suit your specific work environment and context.

The Principles and Methodologies of PBL

The principles and methodologies of PBL can enhance employee performance, foster a culture of continuous learning, and promote innovative problem-solving. This book explores the reasons why and the various points at which we can apply PBL in the work environment, highlighting its benefits and potential impact.

Encouraging Active Learning

By applying PBL in the work environment, employers can shift from traditional training methods to active learning approaches. Instead of passive lectures or instruction, employees engage in problem-solving activities that require critical thinking and active participation. This promotes a deeper understanding of concepts and enhances the application of knowledge in practical scenarios.

Developing Problem-Solving Skills

PBL methodologies focus on developing effective problem-solving skills. In the work environment, employees often encounter complex challenges that require analytical thinking, creative problem-solving, and collaboration. By applying PBL, employees are exposed to real or simulated problems, allowing them to develop their problem-solving abilities, think critically, and propose innovative solutions.

Enhancing Collaboration and Communication

PBL fosters collaboration and communication skills, which are vital in a work environment that increasingly relies on teamwork and interdisciplinary collaboration. Through group problem-solving activities, employees learn to communicate effectively, share ideas, listen actively, and work collectively towards finding solutions. This cultivates a collaborative work culture and improves team dynamics.

Promoting Continuous Learning

Applying PBL in the work environment promotes a culture of continuous learning. Employees are encouraged to seek knowledge, conduct research, and explore different perspectives to address workplace challenges. This helps employees stay updated with industry trends, enhances their expertise, and fosters a growth mindset that values ongoing development.

Bridging Theory and Practice

PBL facilitates the practical application of theoretical knowledge. By applying PBL in the work environment, employees can bridge the gap between academic learning and practical implementation. This allows for a more seamless transfer of knowledge, as employees can directly apply concepts and theories to real-world situations, leading to enhanced job performance and efficiency.

Fostering Innovation and Creativity

PBL methodologies stimulate innovation and creativity in the work environment. By encouraging employees to solve complex problems, think critically, and explore alternative solutions, organizations foster a culture of innovation. PBL provides a structured framework for employees to think outside the box, generate new ideas, and contribute to organizational growth and success.

Promoting Ownership and Autonomy

PBL empowers employees to take ownership of their learning and problem-solving processes. By applying PBL in the work environment, organizations give employees the autonomy to tackle challenges, make decisions, and take responsibility for their professional development. This promotes a sense of ownership and accountability, leading to increased job satisfaction and engagement.

Improving Employee Engagement and Satisfaction

Applying PBL in the work environment can significantly enhance employee engagement and satisfaction. PBL methodologies provide employees with meaningful and challenging tasks, allowing them to actively participate in problem-solving and decision-making processes. This sense of involvement and contribution fosters job satisfaction, motivation, and overall employee well-being.

Addressing Complex and Dynamic Challenges

The modern work environment is characterized by complex and rapidly evolving challenges. PBL is well-suited for addressing such challenges as it encourages employees to adapt, think critically, and find innovative solutions. By applying PBL, organizations equip employees with the necessary skills to navigate and overcome dynamic work environments effectively.

Encouraging Lifelong Learning and Professional Growth

PBL in the work environment promotes lifelong learning and continuous professional growth. It instills a mindset of curiosity, adaptability, and a willingness to learn and improve. Employees become more proactive in seeking opportunities for development, attending training sessions, and engaging in self-directed learning to enhance their skills and expertise.

Applying Problem-Based Learning in the work environment offers numerous benefits, including active learning, enhanced problem-solving skills, improved collaboration and communication, and a culture of continuous learning and innovation. By implementing PBL methodologies, organizations can empower employees, bridge the gap between theory and practice, and foster a dynamic and engaged workforce. Embracing PBL in the work environment is a strategic investment in employee development, leading to increased productivity, satisfaction, and organizational success in the face of evolving challenges.

Sixty Reasons to Apply PBL in the Workplace

Here are sixty reasons on how applying Problem-Based Learning (PBL) in the work environment can improve organizational performance and bottom-line:

1. Enhances critical thinking skills among employees.
2. Fosters a culture of innovation and creative problem-solving.
3. Improves employee engagement and satisfaction.
4. Increases employee motivation and morale.
5. Promotes teamwork and collaboration.
6. Develops effective communication skills within the organization.
7. Encourages knowledge sharing and cross-functional learning.
8. Facilitates continuous learning and professional growth.
9. Reduces employee turnover and increases retention.
10. Enhances adaptability and agility in a rapidly changing business environment.
11. Improves decision-making processes by considering diverse perspectives.
12. Builds a problem-solving mindset across the organization.
13. Enables employees to take ownership of their work and contribute to organizational success.

14. Enhances employee job performance and productivity.
15. Reduces reliance on external consultants for problem-solving.
16. Increases organizational efficiency by addressing challenges in a timely manner.
17. Boosts employee morale and job satisfaction, leading to higher employee loyalty.
18. Develops a learning culture that supports organizational development.
19. Aligns employee goals and organizational objectives.
20. Improves employee problem-solving skills and ability to handle complex challenges.
21. Enhances adaptability to industry and market changes.
22. Increases employee accountability and responsibility.
23. Promotes a proactive and self-directed approach to learning.
24. Facilitates effective knowledge transfer and retention within the organization.
25. Improves organizational agility in responding to customer needs.

26. Builds a shared understanding of organizational goals and challenges.
27. Encourages employees to think critically and challenge assumptions.
28. Promotes a culture of continuous improvement and innovation.
29. Enhances employee autonomy and decision-making capabilities.
30. Stimulates employee creativity and generates new ideas for business growth.
31. Develops employees' leadership and problem-solving skills for future roles.
32. Enhances employee adaptability in an increasingly digital and technology-driven world.
33. Encourages cross-functional collaboration and knowledge exchange.
34. Facilitates the identification and resolution of operational inefficiencies.
35. Increases employee job satisfaction through meaningful and challenging work.
36. Improves the quality of products and services through systematic problem-solving.

37. Enhances employee motivation by involving them in decision-making processes.
38. Boosts employee confidence and self-efficacy.
39. Encourages a proactive approach to continuous learning and development.
40. Enables the organization to respond effectively to industry disruptions.
41. Builds a culture of continuous improvement and continuous learning.
42. Enhances employee engagement in organizational initiatives and projects.
43. Improves customer satisfaction by addressing their needs effectively.
44. Reduces costs associated with recurring problems and inefficiencies.
45. Increases employee loyalty and reduces turnover costs.
46. Promotes a positive and inclusive work environment.
47. Enhances employee problem-solving skills in complex and ambiguous situations.
48. Facilitates knowledge sharing and collaboration across departments and teams.

49. Improves organizational resilience by developing adaptable employees.
50. Enables the organization to capitalize on emerging opportunities.
51. Enhances organizational reputation and brand image.
52. Improves employee retention through increased job satisfaction and growth opportunities.
53. Drives continuous learning and development at all levels of the organization.
54. Increases employee ownership and accountability for organizational outcomes.
55. Facilitates effective change management processes.
56. Promotes a culture of evidence-based decision-making.
57. Improves organizational efficiency and resource allocation.
58. Encourages a culture of curiosity and exploration.
59. Builds a talent pipeline by developing future leaders within the organization.

60. Enhances overall organizational performance and bottom-line results.

These sixty reasons highlight the wide-ranging benefits of applying Problem-Based Learning in the work environment, positively impacting organizational performance, employee engagement, and the bottom line. By embracing PBL, organizations can foster a culture of continuous learning, critical thinking, and collaboration, driving success and growth in today's dynamic business landscape.

Problem-Based Learning (PBL) Application in Departments Within an Organization

Problem-Based Learning (PBL) can be applied to various functions within an organization, including accounting, finance, human resources, strategic management, marketing, project management, and supply chain management. Here are some ways PBL can improve these specific functions:

1. **Accounting:**

- Develops critical thinking skills in analyzing financial data and identifying potential issues or discrepancies.
- Enhances problem-solving abilities in complex accounting scenarios.
- Promotes a deeper understanding of accounting principles through practical application in real-world situations.
- Facilitates collaboration and communication among accounting teams to address accounting challenges effectively.
- Encourages continuous learning and staying updated with changing accounting standards and regulations.

2. **Finance:**

- Develops analytical skills in evaluating financial data and making informed financial decisions.
- Enhances problem-solving abilities in financial planning, budgeting, and forecasting.

- Encourages strategic thinking and analysis of financial risks and opportunities.
- Fosters collaboration between finance and other departments to align financial strategies with organizational goals.
- Promotes a comprehensive understanding of financial markets and instruments through practical problem-solving exercises.

3. Human Resources:

- Develops critical thinking skills in addressing complex HR challenges such as talent acquisition, retention, and development.
- Enhances problem-solving abilities in designing effective HR policies and practices.
- Encourages collaboration and communication among HR teams and other departments for effective talent management.
- Promotes a culture of continuous learning and professional development within the HR function.

- Facilitates the application of HR strategies to real-world scenarios and organizational challenges.

4. **Strategic Management:**

- Develops analytical and critical thinking skills in analyzing industry trends, competitive landscapes, and strategic opportunities.
- Enhances problem-solving abilities in formulating and implementing strategic initiatives.
- Encourages collaboration and communication among cross-functional teams in strategic decision-making.
- Fosters a holistic understanding of business environments and the alignment of organizational strategies.
- Promotes continuous evaluation and adjustment of strategic plans based on real-world challenges and opportunities.

5. Marketing:

- Develops analytical skills in understanding consumer behavior, market trends, and competitive landscapes.
- Enhances problem-solving abilities in developing marketing strategies and campaigns.
- Encourages collaboration and communication among marketing teams to address marketing challenges effectively.
- Promotes creativity and innovation in developing marketing solutions to reach target audiences.
- Facilitates the application of marketing concepts in real-world scenarios, such as product launches or market expansion.

6. Project Management:

- Develops critical thinking skills in planning, executing, and managing projects.

- Enhances problem-solving abilities in identifying and resolving project-related issues and risks.
- Encourages collaboration and communication among project teams and stakeholders.
- Promotes effective project scope and timeline management through practical application.
- Fosters a comprehensive understanding of project management methodologies and best practices.

7. Supply Chain Management:

- Develops analytical skills in optimizing supply chain processes and identifying potential bottlenecks or inefficiencies.
- Enhances problem-solving abilities in managing supply chain disruptions and risks.
- Encourages collaboration and communication among supply chain teams and external partners.
- Promotes a comprehensive understanding of supply chain dynamics and strategic sourcing decisions.

- Facilitates the application of supply chain concepts in real-world scenarios, such as demand forecasting or inventory management.

Overall, Problem-Based Learning in these functions helps develop critical thinking, problem-solving, collaboration, and communication skills, leading to improved performance, better decision-making, and effective management of challenges in each respective area. It fosters a practical and experiential learning approach that aligns theory with real-world applications, enabling professionals to excel in their roles and contribute to organizational success.

US and Inter'l Universities Implemented PBL

Problem-based learning (PBL) is an educational approach that focuses on solving real-world problems as a means of learning. Several universities around the world have adopted PBL as part of their curriculum. Here are some top universities known for implementing problem-based learning:

1. Maastricht University, Netherlands: Maastricht University is renowned for its Problem-Based Learning approach across various disciplines, including medicine, business, and social sciences.
2. McMaster University, Canada: McMaster University in Canada is recognized for its problem-based medical curriculum, known as the McMaster model, which has been widely adopted by medical schools globally.
3. Aalborg University, Denmark: Aalborg University follows a problem-based and project-based learning approach across its engineering programs, emphasizing

real-world problem-solving and collaboration.
4. Case Western Reserve University, United States: Case Western Reserve University's medical school implements PBL as a central component of its curriculum, focusing on small-group discussions and case-based learning.
5. University of Delaware, United States: The University of Delaware's Institute for Transforming Undergraduate Education (ITUE) emphasizes problem-based and experiential learning approaches in various disciplines.
6. University of Hong Kong, Hong Kong: The University of Hong Kong integrates PBL into its medical curriculum, emphasizing active learning, critical thinking, and problem-solving skills development.

More US and international universities known for using Problem-Based Learning (PBL) in their educational programs:

1. University of Newcastle, Australia

2. University of Manchester, United Kingdom
3. Erasmus University Rotterdam, Netherlands
4. Lund University, Sweden
5. University of Toronto, Canada
6. University of Queensland, Australia
7. Karolinska Institute, Sweden
8. Radboud University, Netherlands
9. University of Twente, Netherlands
10. University of Glasgow, United Kingdom
11. University of Helsinki, Finland
12. University of Cape Town, South Africa
13. University of Sydney, Australia
14. University of Auckland, New Zealand
15. Stanford University, United States
16. Harvard University, United States
17. Yale University, United States
18. University of California, San Francisco, United States
19. Massachusetts Institute of Technology (MIT), United States
20. University of Pennsylvania, United States
21. University of California, Los Angeles (UCLA), United States
22. Johns Hopkins University, United States

23. University of California, San Diego, United States
24. University of Washington, United States
25. University of Michigan, United States
26. University of Chicago, United States
27. University of Wisconsin-Madison, United States
28. University of North Carolina at Chapel Hill, United States
29. Duke University, United States
30. Columbia University, United States
31. University of Illinois at Urbana-Champaign, United States
32. University of Colorado Denver, United States
33. University of Pittsburgh, United States
34. University of Utah, United States
35. University of California, Irvine, United States
36. University of California, Berkeley, United States
37. Boston University, United States
38. Northwestern University, United States
39. University of California, Davis, United States
40. University of Minnesota Twin Cities, United States

41. University of Maryland, College Park, United States
42. Georgetown University, United States
43. University of Massachusetts Amherst, United States
44. University of Virginia, United States

References

Albanese, M. A., & Mitchell, S. (1993). Problem-based learning: a review of literature on its outcomes and implementation issues. Academic Medicine, 68(1), 52-81.

Barrows, H. S. (1986). A taxonomy of problem-based learning methods. Medical education, 20(6), 481-486.

Barrows, H. S. (2000). Problem-based learning applied to medical education. Southern Illinois University School of Medicine.

Boud, D., & Feletti, G. (1997). The challenge of problem-based learning (2nd ed.). Kogan Page.

Colliver, J. A. (2000). Effectiveness of problem-based learning curricula: Research and theory. Academic Medicine, 75(3), 259-266.

Dochy, F., Segers, M., Van den Bossche, P., & Gijbels, D. (2003). Effects of problem-based learning: a meta-analysis. Learning and Instruction, 13(5), 533-568.

Dolmans, D. H., Loyens, S. M., Marcq, H., & Gijbels, D. (2016). Deep and surface learning in problem-based learning: a review of the literature. Advances in Health Sciences Education, 21(5), 1087-1112.

Dolmans, D. H., Wolfhagen, I. H., & van der Vleuten, C. P. (2001). Solving problems with group work in problem-based learning: What do we know? Medical Teacher, 23(4), 459-465.

Dolmans, D. H., Wolfhagen, I. H., van der Vleuten, C. P., & Wijnen, W. H. (2001). Solving problems with group work in problem-based learning: hold on to the philosophy. Medical teacher, 23(4), 358-363.

Gijselaers, W. H., Schmidt, H. G., & van der Vleuten, C. P. (Eds.). (1995). Educational innovation in economics and business administration: The case of problem-based learning. Springer.

Hmelo-Silver, C. E. (2004). Problem-based learning: What and how do students learn? Educational Psychology Review, 16(3), 235-266.

Hmelo-Silver, C. E. (2004). Problem-based learning: What lies ahead? In T. L. Good (Ed.), 21st Century Education: A Reference Handbook (Vol. 2, pp. 225-233). SAGE Publications.

Hmelo-Silver, C. E., Duncan, R. G., & Chinn, C. A. (2007). Scaffolding and achievement in problem-based and inquiry learning: A response to Kirschner, Sweller, and Clark (2006). Educational Psychologist, 42(2), 99-107.

Hung, W. (2008). The 4C/ID model: A comprehensive approach for designing instruction. Educational Technology Research and Development, 56(4), 385-407.

Hung, W. (2009). The 9-step problem design process for problem-based learning:

application of the 3C3R model. Educational Research Review, 4(2), 118-141.

Kaufman, D. M., & Mann, K. V. (1999). Comparing achievement on the Medical Council of Canada qualifying examination Part I of students in conventional and problem-based learning curricula. Academic Medicine, 74(10 Suppl.), S86-S88.

Maudsley, G., & Strivens, J. (2000). Promoting professional knowledge, experiential learning and critical thinking for medical students. Medical Education, 34(7), 535-544.

Norman, G. (2015). Problem-based learning: The problem of assessment. Medical Education, 49(6), 588-592.

Norman, G. R., & Schmidt, H. G. (1992). The psychological basis of problem-based learning: a review of the evidence. Academic Medicine, 67(9), 557-565.

Savery, J. R., & Duffy, T. M. (1996). Problem based learning: An instructional model and its constructivist framework. Educational technology, 35(5), 31-38.

Savin-Baden, M. (2003). Facilitating problem-based learning: Illuminating perspectives. Open University Press.

Savin-Baden, M., & Wilkie, K. (2003). Problem-based learning in higher education: Untold stories. SRHE and Open University Press.

Schmidt, H. G., & Moust, J. H. (1995). Factors affecting small-group tutorial learning: A review of research. In H. G. Schmidt, & M. L. De Volder (Eds.), Tutorials in problem-based learning: A new direction in teaching the health professions (pp. 79-92). Springer.

Schmidt, H. G., Rotgans, J. I., & Yew, E. H. J. (2011). The process of problem-based learning: what works and why. Medical Education, 45(8), 792-806.

Strobel, J., & van Barneveld, A. (2009). When is PBL more effective? A meta-synthesis of meta-analyses comparing PBL to conventional classrooms. Interdisciplinary Journal of Problem-Based Learning, 3(1), 44-58.

Torp, L., & Sage, S. (2002). Problems as possibilities: Problem-based learning for K-16 education. Alexandria, VA: ASCD.

Vernon, D. T., & Blake, R. L. (1993). Does problem-based learning work? A meta-analysis of evaluative research. Academic medicine, 68(7), 550-563.

Wilkerson, L., & Gijselaers, W. (1996). Bringing problem-based learning to higher education: Theory and practice. New Directions for Teaching and Learning, 1996(68), 3-11.

Williams, B., & Llewellyn, D. (2007). Problem-based learning in undergraduate paramedic education: Towards a conceptual framework. BMC Medical Education, 7(1), 1-9.

Printed in Poland
by Amazon Fulfillment
Poland Sp. z o.o., Wrocław